WHY NOT ME?

A Transformative Introspection and Reflection in the Throes of Life's Challenges, Priming Life's Worth, Not Net Worth

Adeyombo Aderinto

Acknowledgement

To my great-grandparents, grandparents, parents, and the extended family: I tender my homage to a lineage that continues to inspire me daily. To Helen, my love, for your unceasing care during my health crises, my gratitude swells every time I think of you. To friends and others I have crossed paths with, thank you for your influence, whether as positive examples or lessons from non-examples, both of which have shaped my journey. To Tayo Popoola, my uncle Dr. Daniel Ogunjumo, and Grace Nsor, thank you for being avid readers of my manuscripts; thank you for lending me your eyes, ears, and minds. To my young learners, you humanize me every day, and I'm a better person for that. Thank you all. I am forever swaddled in your protective apparel — your humanity.

Table of Contents

Why Not Me? - Foreword

Life is fascinating as it presents itself in many forms that allow us to learn and grow while being tested by challenges. Everything within our individual or shared orbit allows us to reshape our existence for our own betterment—to rethink, redo, and refresh as we grow, reflecting life's dynamism. Oftentimes, there are cues or prompts in our lives that point us toward change, which we mostly ignore or fail to heed, until maybe later in life when a massive, life-threatening hardship comes our way. It was so for me recently when I was jarringly tested by cancer. It was a huge challenge to face. It was urgent and sparked a life-changing awakening in me.

"Why Not Me?" (this book) unveils how I'm now distilling substance from sludge in my quest for growth to be a better version of myself, one who is at peace with the self, in harmony with others and nature; one who accepts that life is not in full bloom without challenges; one whose resolve, spirituality, and faith are not suspect; one who doesn't wallow in victimhood, the perceived unfairness of life or its inauspiciousness; and one who asks, "Why not me?" rather than

"Why me?", with the understanding that, as humans, we are a repository of resources to take on life's challenges that can eventually lead to growth and desirable fulfillment. This kind of growth or fulfillment is becoming increasingly uncommon in today's world; it is non-material, straightforward, and basic. It is a "life worth," not "net worth," achievable with spirituality (not the popular type), believing in the self, benevolence, faith, connection with nature, and our creator. Life is the ultimate gift, and it behooves us to give it back the way it's given to us. As espoused by the Dalai Lama, "It is a miracle to be born at all. So, what are you going to do with your life?"

Through this journey of transformation in this book, I have drawn from an assortment of experiences, mine and others', to create a life's worth as opposed to a net worth, something that may not appeal to all of us but is a metric for a supreme life. For me, it is personal, as it is a schema to make adjustments for pursuing my life's worth. Regrets are hardly what we think they are; they form the basis of instructive lessons in our lives, just as failure negates itself to pave the way for learning and growth.

Front and center in this book is the influence of my great-grandparents, my grandparents, and others, including children, who have been a great resource in my journey of self-discovery, self-affirmation, and pursuit of life's worth.

While this is primarily personal, I have drawn on the experiences of the people around me and those of icons among us to tame my subjective views. I have also offered multiple perspectives from others on specific aspects of the book as a way for me or all of us to learn and grow.

In sum, the touchstone for me in all of this is the moments before my grandfather took his last breath. He had been comatose for a few months and hadn't opened his eyes or said anything to anyone. Suddenly, one day, he opened his eyes, smiled broadly, and remarked, "The world is a market. Your worth is what you show and sell. It's been good." Seconds later, according to accounts, life vacated his shell. He could tell that he had dignified his sojourn here on Earth. He found bliss. May you find meaning beyond the pages of this book that will yield your life's worth. Transcendence!

Adeyombo

The Rupture: Far From Rapture

Foot-tapping on a hardwood floor while sitting, I looked around and was not alone. There were others, mostly men in their fifties or older. They were not physically feeble and not visibly troubled. Some were chatting with family members who were there for and with them. The context appeared normal, but it wasn't. It felt calm, but it was far from it. My emotions were rumbling, far removed from calm, and with fear mostly tipping the scale. I briefly took a mental trip out of the room to escape the moment, experiencing random flashbacks of my childhood, adolescence, and recent adulthood. I was in a reverie far distant from the future. Unburdened and unbothered, I was not present in the moment for a few minutes. Then I faintly heard my name; it was a call for me to step to the window for check-in. Although I dreaded the call, it was necessary. I cleared check-in and was in the waiting room a few minutes later. "The doctor is ready for you now," a medically uniformed lady said. I followed her into an endless hallway, and it seemed I could not accelerate my strides enough to quicken the moment. As they always say, time is relative, as a few steps took longer than the time I could spare. I wanted to know, good or bad! "Here," the uniformed lady said, gesturing me into the room. Then, I saw him. He shook my hand and spoke a few words that did not resonate with my emotions. Although I heard him, my internal turmoil overpowered the intent and meaning of his words. Even now, I am not sure if I responded cordially to his goodwill. I saw him indicate the chair in front of his massive desk for me to sit in. "Now, let's see," he said, looking at the screen and clicking away. His face creased slightly, and my heart raced. It must not be good, I thought. A long pause followed, with the man's face somberly glued to the screen. "You are young and don't look like something is wrong with you. Well, we've got cancer here." Dead silence! The two-syllabled word sounded anathema to my being. It was nothing short of doom, the end! "That's it," I muttered on that distant horizon far beyond the earthly skies. There, I felt I could transcend death, escapism to avoid the moment.

Seconds later, I faintly heard the man's voice on the other side of the screen, "What do you want to do?" There was that lull again on my part, as I was not an expert in this case. "What options do we have?" I asked. Then I heard his printer kick in. He collected the printed pages and moved to the side of the desk to show me the results of the biopsy he had done a week or two before. "This is the extent of what we have now," said the doctor. "You asked for options, and we have a few. We can do chemotherapy and hope for the best. We can have surgery and buy you another 15 to 20 years, although it is not guaranteed. We can also try other things to see if cancer will reverse its course." I have heard people use stages to describe the ruthlessness of cancer, and it occurred to me that this could give me an inkling of what I was facing. "What stage cancer is this?" I asked. Not looking at me and rifling through some documents on his desk, he said, "Stage 1 or 2. It's between those two numbers." Stage 4, I knew, would deny me any glimmer of hope. A bit sanguine, I asked which option would be best. "Well, we can cut and hopefully kill it in its early stages," he said. "Well, then, let's do it. How about next week?" I asked. "Not that soon. We still have a few steps to get to surgery. "How long?" I asked again. "Give or take five weeks because we have tests and other things to run," he explained. Detecting the urgency and desperation in my voice and questions, he gave me April 17, 2025, for surgery conditionally, only if everything turned out well with the tests. That triggered my feelings of forlornness again: the surgery might not even happen as scheduled. I looked through the vast expanse of the doctor's window on this cloudless day, way beyond the present. The world was beyond the window, but I was not in it. My situation here was frustratingly restrictive: I could only see things wistfully without room for participation.

The doctor's voice brought me back to reality. "Well, let us hope for the best. Get through those tests, and we'll see what happens." He directed me to his front office, where they handed me pre-surgery papers, including referrals to other doctors. My world plunged and entered a new phase, an unforeseen, unsavory, and unwelcome one with which I must deal. What do I do now? Who do I tell? Where do I go? It was a cascade of questions I had to answer to contend with my new and real world. Leaving the doctor's office, I realized that my gait had more bounce, my smiles had more ease, and my overall aura had more verve and good-naturedness. I greeted everyone I saw effortlessly. I bantered lightly and delighted in people's good vibes.

The elevator ride downstairs allowed me to decide who to tell, indeed, not many people by my nature. I tend to be more private with my agonies and challenges than my highs and celebrations. Bringing other people's attention to my hardship is inconsiderate, I think. Many people around me have resented this attitude for years, often miffed that I do not value their friendship or relationship with me as much as they do mine. Not so! The real reason a relationship should not be exploited by burdening others with one's problems is that people generally have their challenges, which might be more constraining or harsher than what one is going through. I appreciate people's time, but I reluctantly take it when offered. It is much easier for me to give my time than to take someone else's. I hardly feel any inconvenience when asked to help. What I feel is a mix of excitement and elation. I see a wonderful opportunity when people ask me to help, which, in my case, often leads to learning and growth. I have learned many valuable lessons in life by doing things for other people.

The walk between the elevator and the garage helped me clear my head about whom I should tell at this early stage. My wife must know, and so must my sister. However, I felt I should break it down to them in bits, small doses. I would first tell them about having to be biopsied. I thought this would somehow soften the news of the cancer finding. For everyone else, the narrow-release approach would also apply. I would scale it back so as not to burden them with my emotions or impose my predicament on them while they grapple with their own.

Again, this attitude of mine, not to cause panic or bother people, has been frowned upon by family members and friends for some time now. "Let us know when you need something, or there's a problem," some would say. Others would feel slighted if I did not make them aware of my struggles, to the point that they might see me as arrogant. It is not arrogance; it is not a cover-up. It is a way to bear my cross and lighten the weight of others' crosses. I am faltering and still struggling with this so-called flaw, to the displeasure of my closest friends and family.

Once I resolved the problem of who to tell, I had to determine my next destination; home was not it. Home now seemed dreary and desolate, completely different from what I had known, given my new reality. I did not drown myself in dreariness, though. If anything, acceptance, couched in optimism, took hold of me. I became more aware of my environment: people, cars, the sky, hills, and the sun, all visual and auditory. I thought that all that was present, the ambiance, would be the same the next day, and that I would be a part of the interplay. I exited the garage, still unsure of where to go. In a flash, I yielded to my instincts and decided to do something salving or relieving in my area of interest.

It was a beautiful, bright, temperate California morning that oozed joy and good vibes, and I was swaddled in it as I got into the car. Home was not the place to be, for it might incite dejection or morbidity. I wanted to escape the specter of lifelessness. I needed to be where my emotions, far away from my current dilemma, would flow freely, granting me the quintessence of being, my happiest state, a state of calm and unburdened being.

Unmindfully, I drove off the street onto one of the freeways nearby. North, south, west, or east, it did not matter. Just being on the freeway was good enough. Somehow, I realized that the freeway I was on had often taken me to places of my special interests, things for which I have a swelling passion. I love the arts in all their forms,

and on this day, home designs and decorative accessories were what

helped me ward off my melancholic feelings. The thought of it alone

was an opportunity to create a short-term focus that would not

deplete my energy but rather ground me in a state of calm and poise.

I found my way to a huge design center for home furnishings and

decorative accessories, a place I had often visited. The intention was

not to buy but to browse and appreciate designs and creativity. When

I am in a space that features art and design, I feel psychologically

buoyant and unrestrained and can create my own space of bliss and

aesthetics. That aesthetic sensibility led me to the design center on

this day.

I sauntered in without any emotional baggage, nothing to wear me

out or weigh me down like the new cancer alert I had just received.

The environment, my passion, and my interest caused this benign

diversion. I went from floor to floor and examined assorted items,

identifying what I could purchase and envisioning how to utilize

them. I became indifferent to the threat of cancer, resolutely

oblivious to its notoriety for ravaging or stealing lives. Strongly, I told myself that cancer would have no place in my small world. There was that feeling of ease, calm, and congeniality as I walked the floors of the design center. For some reason, I unusually beamed and said hello to shoppers I made eye contact with, and they responded similarly. The mutuality or commonality in our being at the design center perhaps was the reason we all felt at ease with one another. As I was checking out the items, a young man who was also shopping said, "You look great! I like your style." I thanked him for the compliment and continued browsing. Then, minutes later, it happened again; with a smile, a female shopper in her late twenties said, " Hi there! You look sharp. Anything happening?" I thanked her and said that nothing special was happening and that it was just me on a workday. Facetiously, she said it would be nice to help her husband shop for clothes. We laughed, she moved on, and I returned to browsing the decor items. For a moment, I pondered why people were exchanging niceties with me. Did they see death in my eyes and want to be nice?

Somehow, the two compliments stayed with me as I looked at different items. What made these two people compliment me directly? What was special about what I was wearing that day? After all, a pair of black jeans, a T-shirt, a jacket, and a pair of dress or tennis shoes were my fashion staples. In the vein of fashion, that day was my every day. Nothing special! However, these two people saw something I took for granted as an enhancement. Playing in my head were all kinds of thoughts. For example, would these two shoppers have freely or generously offered their compliments if they had known that a death sentence had been handed to me two hours before? After all, death is more sinisterly profound and significant than style, fashion, or anything else. At first, I thought there were no benefits to the compliments since I could die. Then came a twist in my thoughts. I began to see the expressed admiration of the two shoppers, among many other things, as a validation of who I was, my identity, my psyche, and my general outlook, even in the face of death. I did not see any need to give this part of me up when threats came knocking. I could only fight and dignify myself, even in the face of defeat, with the little I had that could help my chance of survival. The plaudits or validation given to me by the two shoppers were a defining factor in what I had, even though they might have

seemed popularly insignificant.

Filtering all these thoughts, I decided that I would not be drowned in

dreariness, thinking about cancer and death. I would be intact or

even better in my thoughts and deeds. I would be more aware of

each moment in a way that allowed me to learn more and appreciate

outcomes, good or bad. I would realize that whatever we see or deem

as bad may well be the very thing that begets what is good. Life is

not linear and does not always present fluidly. It flexes, and so must

we. I just had to adapt. My optimism was short-term, not long-term,

for I might not live past the April 17 surgery date. It could also be

that I would not come out of surgery alive. It could also happen that

I would make it through surgery. Either way, I was okay. In all of

this, though, I did not stop thinking about the future. I reflected on

my special-interest projects, what I wanted to be doing in two years,

where I would like to be, and how I could be effective in my

relationships with those in my sphere of influence. I particularly

thought about how I should not let any setbacks close my eyes and mind to the brightness around me, for that brightness could be the

energy for hope and triumph.

Andrea: An Angel in Abstract?

As I was readjusting to my dilemma, thinking about how to be strong, be myself, and cope or transcend it, I remembered that two months earlier, before my cancer diagnosis, a ten-year-old girl had given me a wooden cross about the size of my palm. That cross would become a source of hope, faith, spirituality, and protection for me, perhaps as intended by the ten-year-old who gave it to me.

Andrea, the ten-year-old, presents with autism as established by her school district and other specialty agencies. As a learning strategist and learning disabilities specialist, I work with children who have learning challenges, utilizing various resources and strategies to make learning accessible and achievable. I have been doing this with and for Andrea for almost three years now.

Andrea has characteristics and traits that differ from those that can be observed in her peers. She is private and keeps to herself; she is persistent, insistent, and rigid in her interests, and she subtly and consistently shows empathy. She derives joy from illustrating and drawing and can do so all day. Her drawings are one way she shows what she is thinking and knows. For example, writing becomes easier for her when she uses her drawings to express herself. When she is awake or alert, she is unceasingly busy. She is always doing something, drawing, using her laptop, or listening to music. She can do all or any of these without missing anyone's company. However, she occasionally banters with one or two students she feels safe with. There is one student whom she enjoys being with. This student, another ten-year-old, is diligent, dedicated, responsible, and studious. She is also mild-mannered and empathetic. Andrea takes directions and redirections very well from this student, perhaps because of the student's sincerity regarding her intent and actions. They are always busy together and hardly disagree to the extent of anger or resentment.

I spend a lot of time observing her to determine how I can best support her in achieving her goals. I provide context for her interests and use these to get to know her better. Andrea, I have discovered, has a sense of humor that, once stoked, can make her laugh animatedly and delightfully. She enjoys silly, nonsensical things and is quick to see absurdities in situations, which often helps her to be humorous. When Andrea is at a breakdown point, for example, I employ humor to defuse a tense circumstance for her. She loves music, and I give her time to enjoy it after completing her tasks or work. Andrea is fast with the laptop and knows how to use multiple apps.

Watching her work efficiently on the laptop is fascinating. A born naturalist, she excitedly looks for articles and stories about animals using her computer. She has pets at home, takes care of them, and often shares stories about them with her few friends. This naturalist disposition and her empathetic sense are a significant part of who she is: content, disciplined in terms of what she wants and what she wants to do, and never idling in her privacy. She is genuine and unpretentious. She is a friend, and by how she responds to me, she sees me as a friend, too. Our friendship is mutual.

I have always known for a while now that Andrea is a friend, a special person who thinks about you even when there is no contact or when she is away. There is something about her that's spiritual and innocent; it is purity. An unexpected incident would mark this purity or spirituality in January of 2025.

Andrea: An Angel in Abstract?

It was the first day of school following winter recess, and I was ready for my routine as a specialist who works with students and educators to address learning challenges and develop effective strategies. I was mindful of my objectives on this day and was focused on meeting all of them. I was beaming as I saw each familiar face of the students, cognizant of how much I had missed this entire community of learners and educators.

From the moment I left the parking lot, it was going to be a happy morning, so I proceeded upstairs to my room to start the day in a bubbly way. There, waiting for me at the door, were Andrea and her mother. "Hey, Andrea, welcome back. Did you have a good break?" I asked. Andrea did not say a word but started to rummage through her backpack hurriedly. Within seconds, she gleefully brought out a wooden cross about the size of my palm. "Here, this is for you, for your protection," she said. "For me?" I queried rhetorically. "She saved her money and got it for you," said the mother. Before I could even express my gratitude to Andrea, she had walked away in her shuffling style. That was Andrea, a person who would dismiss the importance of her deeds or sacrifice at the expense of her own gratification. She wanted nothing back from me, not even words of gratitude. This was a purity of intent. This meant a great deal to me and added significant value to her person. Somehow, I felt that what she had given me was not an ordinary cross; it was a special and spiritual essence. Why would this kid, of all the things she could have given me, get me a cross? Why did she think about me away from the context of our academic relationship? Why did she think that I would need protection? I had many more questions and often wondered if her gesture was foreshadowing a future need for the cross or protection. My feelings about the cross became overwhelming, and I began to think of it as having a purpose or role in my life. I decided not to part with the cross, considering its latent significance or purpose. I remember telling friends about the spirituality surrounding this special gift and clear-mindedly pledging to keep the cross in my possession and in my mind, as things could happen that would warrant protection. I had that presentiment that something would happen, and it did.

The Onset of Rupture, Acceptance, and Optimism

In January 2025, I returned to my urologist to review the results of the blood test I had recently undergone. Normally, I would see my primary doctor every three months, but in the case of the urologist, I had skipped four of five sessions of follow-up. The last time I saw him before 2025 was in 2023, with a PSA score of 4.2, a three-point jump from 1.2, which was within normal limits in 2022. In January of 2025, following another test, my urologist was alarmed by how rapidly my PSA was rising. This time, it was 6.4, five points above my best reading. Without mincing words, my doctor raised a red flag and suggested we undergo a biopsy. Seeing how concerned he was and how disturbingly my PSA had jumped, I gave myself up for a biopsy. It was done, and two weeks later, it was confirmed that I had early-stage cancer. To me, cancer was cancer, a death sentence, early or late-stage. Any degree of it, I thought, was distasteful or life-ending.

A biopsy is just one part of pre-surgery preparation. As a patient, as opposed to being an expert, I thought a biopsy was all that we would have to do before surgery, not so! To be more accurate about the diagnosis, my doctor ordered a few more tests and screenings, including a CT scan, nuclear imaging, EKG, and other general clearances in preparation for surgery. Each procedure was emotional and grounded me in the reality of my health dilemma. I could not outright create relieving diversions, even when I tried. It was relentlessly haunting, more so when I had to do something related to the diagnosis. My CT scan, for example, was emotionally grueling.

The machine alone was ominous; it had a deathly semblance to it. It was like a coffin, a permanent encasement for one's breathless body. I did not like it and felt uncomfortable. I was placed on the slider in a supine position, like in a coffin, and this became an imposing imagery for me, suggesting death, funeral, singing, tributes, and more. To ward off this elegiac imagery, I defaulted to sleeping while the scan was going on, thinking at least that would dispense with the specter of death, at least in this context. The scan began, and I was able to drift away from the process, although my mind remained alert to the environment. With my eyes closed and ears open, I was able to imagine and hear what was going on. I felt the slider move and briefly stop many times as the machine performed its programmed duty.

I could tell that the technicians were examining my inner anatomy on the screen. What would they find aside from cancer? Could the cancer have metastasized? Would I leave the room with hope or despair? The questions went on endlessly, more frighteningly than comforting. In my eagerness to know my fate, I began attaching meaning to every word spoken by the technicians. One word I heard, "tumor," instantly darkened the room and my world. "Do I make the spots darker?" one of the two technicians asked, talking to the lead radiologist. I panicked, thinking that the words "tumor" and "dark spots" suggested that my cancer was deadlier than I had thought. I managed to sneak a peek at the CT screen and, indeed, saw spots. "Another type of cancer? I am going to die," I mused.

I felt a harrowing urge to ask the technicians what my chances of survival were, but I could not, for fear that death could be confirmed for me. I began to think I would walk out of the room in a worse shape than when I entered it. If death had been miles away from me before I entered the CT room, it was now closer, just around the corner. Suddenly, in a mind-over-matter mode, I felt the resurgence of acceptance again, mindful that there was nothing I could do about it if it was meant to be. Preordained! Almost immediately, panic yielded to calm. Despair gave way to gratitude for being here, while others— perhaps younger, better, more faithful, more brilliant, more talented, or more useful to humanity—have departed this world. I could have been taken at a younger age, plagued by an excruciating and insidious disease, or outright wiped out in an accident. I might not have made it through childbirth, I might not have been lucky to be there on my very first day of school, or I might not have been fortunate enough to have sixty-six months of May successively here on Earth. Anything could have happened, for nothing in life was assured or guaranteed. Reflecting on all this allowed me to rationalize my dilemma more realistically and fearlessly. Why not me? And so, it did not matter anymore that the word "tumor" was said, nor did the spots on the screen scare me. Whatever happened was my lot, and I was ready to embrace it. I had considered asking the CT scan personnel about my chances, but it was unnecessary, as it would not have changed anything. "All done. You did well," the radiologist in the room said. I thanked the crew and left the room, wondering what they would say about my scan results once I was out of earshot. Again, it did not matter.

Reasoning and rationalization play a significant role in shaping our emotions, influencing how we perceive and respond to things that sadden or delight us. What I have come to realize over the years is that accepting and acknowledging a problem or dilemma unveils a pathway to realistic and practical solutions. In other words, the first step in the problem-solving process is owning the problem itself.

In line with my belief that owning a problem is beneficial, opposites are complementary. When we have two dissimilar things, one defines the other or balances it. In everything in our lives, there are always two sides that are not the same, and we often see one side as benign and the other as malignant; however, it takes both sides to see or think clearly. Illustratively, in the case of optimism and pessimism, which are emotion-based, it takes one to know the other. Hence, in this reality, it makes sense to mind both, knowing fully well that things can turn out in favor of or against you, as outcomes

cannot be vetted or guaranteed, even when you try. Pessimism is an

outright surrender: you give up, do nothing, and ditch hope.

Optimism, on the other hand, is an informed acceptance of a

challenging situation. It accompanies your willingness to make the

necessary efforts to overcome the presenting obstacles while

understanding that the outcome may not be what you desire. Perhaps

leaving a little room for disappointment after trying is a good thing,

after all. If disappointment happens, at least you will have the

satisfaction of trying. This is the kind of mindset that I began to

nurture even before my ordeal with cancer started, and this has

helped me immensely to come to grips with my dilemma. It has

helped me to not necessarily give up, but to maintain a settled mind

about my plight, whether it is favorable or unfavorable. This mindset

fostered peace for me and gave me the courage to persevere and

hope.

It is the same emotional process that underlies what I now describe

as the relative rationalization process. It is a comparative analysis of

what has happened to others in relation to one's personal experience,

The Onset of Rupture, Acceptance, and Optimism

specifically focusing on how others have not been as fortunate in

similar situations. Doing this allowed me to be more at ease, more

realistic, with my cancer ordeal. "Why not me?" I asked rhetorically,

reminding myself of what other people had gone through that were

worse than mine. I was able to see that my case was better, but it

could have been worse, as others were not as fortunate. Rationally,

this attenuated my fear of death. If others—who were younger,

better, and more useful to the world than me— had been called

home, what place did I have, and what excuses could I offer for

being inactive in my own fate?

Processing and Understanding Death

In flashes, I began to remember those whose death was very traumatic for me because I thought they had died too soon. My very first experience of death was when my great-grandfather died. That was sixty-three years ago, when I was four years old. I knew that people were grim and mournful, but I did not feel any sense of loss. I was only four. I thought my great-grandfather would come back and that I would be in tow, following him, watching him, conversing with him, and being his everyday friend. While he was lying in state, I remember going over to his bedside to look at his cotton-covered eyes because he was not looking at me as he would, nor was he talking to me as he had done before. He was still! I leaned over and tapped his shoulders, but he did not respond. Well, I naively thought that this was not going to be permanent: he would respond in his usual way the next time I tapped him. I walked away from the scene and felt nothing had changed in my life. I thought my great-grandfather would come back. He never did.

Processing and Understanding Death

Years later, in my pre-adolescence, my experience of death took a new turn. I became more attuned to its presence and began to understand its nature better. I began to see death as a loss, a dreariness that could hardly be shaken off, and something that had no filters and was indiscriminate in who it took, why it took them, and when it snatched them.

More mature and better experienced, I began to nurture a better understanding of death with the passing of my aunt. The last of eight children of my grandparents, she was twenty-five years old when she was silenced. She was uniquely successful in all aspects, as a mother, wife, sister, daughter, friend, and professional. Above all, she was an exceptional human being. She had accomplished much for her age and was a hallmark of a fruitful life. She was one whom I was happy with, about, and for, even when I had not seen her or heard from her. She was always there in full grace and grandeur, a person who presented herself in many ways, as an aunt, a friend, and a symbol of human decency.

My aunt loved me and demonstrated this in so many ways. She came to the world eleven years before I did and knew the world better than

I did. She believed it was her role to protect me, ground me morally, and set me straight when I faltered. As a child who was less experienced than her, hers was a role I could not resist because it was much needed in my growth.

Particularly memorable were the times she would take me on long train rides to see my grandparents, her parents, in the northern part of Nigeria. She was sixteen then, and I was four or five years old. The train ride was always at night and lasted nine or ten hours (with stops at various stations) for us to reach Minna, our destination, a city where my grandfather was the administrator of a teacher's college. My grandmother, on the other hand, was a businessperson with multiple businesses in her name, including many bakeries. They lived in a sizable, modern house on a college campus surrounded by rocky hills. There were well-manicured and luxuriant lawns in various areas of the campus, with identical trees flanking both sides of the roadways and branches presenting dense and uniform foliage. There were also fruit trees, including mango and guava, and more, positioned equidistantly throughout various parts of the campus. Even as a child, this setting was aesthetically and psychologically appealing to me. It had the allure of paradise, a serene place where I could roam freely and explore, and where my emotions were not threatened. This was hallowed ground for me, and even now, it is hard for me to separate the splendor of this hallowed ground from the aura and memory of my aunt.

Our trips to see my grandparents always began with a road trip to the town where the train station was located, about thirty miles from our departure point. From the moment I knew we were going to travel, it was pure euphoria being with my aunt. At times, we would travel with my aunt's friends, who were also young, vibrant, and socially savvy. I was the only child among them, but my aunt did not care; she was the only one shepherding a child.

Taking their cues from my aunt, the friends easily conformed to her love and care for me, treating me like she would. I noticed that this happened consistently wherever we went and with whomever we visited. She had a way of integrating me into a circle of adults and letting them know that whatever applied to her in terms of decency and respect also applied to me; my age did not matter. There were no places too plush for both of us to access. Wherever we went, I was always in tow and felt that she was always mindful of my presence— attending to my needs, checking in with me, and ensuring I was comfortable. She was there unfailingly each moment I needed her. I was her priority, and I felt a sense of belonging in the different circles in which we found ourselves. I received a lot of attention from everyone we met, and this soon became another term of endearment for my ties to the group, all under the auspices of my aunt. Although I was a child, I was perceptive enough to know that she was one of the few dearest people in my life.

Beyond her relationship and interactions with me, she was an appealing person with a noticeable flair. She was tall and could be rated ten out of ten in beauty, with long legs and a perfectly set smile. The eyes were narrowly oval and dreamy, almost with an Asian semblance.

Her smile was never insincere; there was always that wellspring of sincerity in and behind it. She was an ardent self-groomer, fashionable, and presentable among her peers. Then there was the brain; she had graduated at the top of her high school class and thereafter took on computer science at the university when computer technology was in its infancy in 1967. She was uncommonly and admirably endowed. She made an impression on me beyond what words and emotions could convey.

It was on the street that the news came to me, about sixty-five miles from her city of residence. I ran into a friend who thought that I had heard about my aunt's passing. He expressed his condolences, but I was not buying them, nor did I believe him, because no one had informed me about her demise. I thought he was talking about someone else, certainly not my dearest aunt. I had to travel home, and I did. It was true; she had departed. At seventeen, life became meaningless for me, as I thought death was unfair. Why her at such an early age with a promising future? Why her, the one who was a friend to everyone and had no enemies? I had many more questions and could not get past my anger with death. She was taken when the lights were bright and shining, and my world darkened. I was in great despair and anger that I thought it should have been me who got taken, not her. Death went too far and eventually became less of a threat to me. Why her? Why not me? Then, there was Lance.

Lance did not feature in my life as my aunt did. He was my high school fellow student. His death, at age seventeen, rent my soul. He was two years ahead of me in high school, but we were remarkably close. He was funny and affable to the core, admired by everyone, and sought after by all. Most memorable was his knack for making people laugh and bringing them happiness. His feel-good aura was one of his master qualities. He was popular with everyone: teachers, friends, our principal, other school personnel, and even students in different high schools in the city.

Lance was about five feet seven inches tall, still growing at seventeen, with a tawny skin and miniature afro haircut. He was inclined to neatness and kept his uniforms and dormitory clothing clean. He was gregarious and genial, but his sense of humor and his knack for creating lighter moments were his most significant values with all the students. Unprompted, he would crack jokes and improvise with funny narratives that were contextual and relevant. He had it all and was everyone's secret envy. Then, one day, Lance disappeared, swallowed by a pond we all thought was a resource for us all. The pond turned on us; it took Lance.

Processing and Understanding Death

It was an unusually overcast weekend day. The clouds were ominously gathering in dark patches, and I felt a bit worried about the somberness, especially when we got to the pond to fetch water for our various needs in the dormitories. We occasionally did this when the public water supply ceased. The pond was the alternate source, and most, if not all, of my schoolmates would converge at the pond to get water. It was so on this day. There must have been about eighty female and male students at the pond, and we all used the opportunity to socialize by bantering, chattering, pranking, and swimming. The swimmers were the ones who got the attention of everyone at the pond, as the youngest three among us, perhaps eleven years old, were the dazzling swimmers. They would sharply dive into the water, disappear for a minute, and reappear a few yards away from where they had plunged. Seeing these younger students flipping and disappearing, only to show up again, gliding gracefully in the water, was quite a spectacle. We all forgot we were there to get water for a long while. We all watched, bedazzled by the swimming skills, especially the acrobatics displayed by the boys. The spectating girls among us were the ones who admired the young swimmers the most; they screamed and applauded in awe of the boys. For a moment, jealous of the boys, I thought about joining the swimmers for the attention they were getting. I wanted the girls to admire me as well. Then I looked at the still, dark, and uninviting water. It gave me chills as I began to wonder about the danger the water could harbor. In my flash imagination, I saw crocodiles, snakes, and even a scary water apparition. With all of this, something was still encouraging me to plunge into the water to garner attention from the girls alongside the young swimmers. Then I looked at the pond again, and I had the premonition that if I got in the water with the boys, I would no longer breathe; I would be dead. I stayed in my spot and continued to watch and cheer. Minutes later, screaming for everyone's attention, Lance dived, and everyone applauded. One, two, three, four, and five minutes later, he was still in the water; we did not see his arms, head, or anything to show us that he was adept at swimming. He did not reappear as the younger swimmers had done. It was now clear that something had gone wrong. Dead silence! The applause ceased, and the cheers became sobs. The young swimmers were urgently back in the water, but this time not for attention. They frantically disappeared in the water to find Lance, and, for a minute or two, the pond was ominously calm amidst mounting sobs. Then there was Lance floating in the hands of the youngest swimmer, all limp and silenced.

"Senior Lance! Senior Lance! Help! Help!" Barlow, the youngest swimmer and the best of them all, cried for help. With foam oozing from his mouth and still limp following thirty minutes of resuscitation efforts, Lance was carried on the shoulders of four students to the nearest roadside, twenty minutes away from the pond. We followed them to the roadside, from where a few students took him to the hospital. We heard an hour later that he never made it. Our school was never the same again without Lance. He was an asset whose value we belittled. We were all deeply hurt. I was immensely numbed by Lance's death at seventeen, so that I thought his departure was unfair and that if he could be taken, I would not cry foul if death had a roster and called me to check out. Death mercilessly did that to Lance. Why not me?

Years later, I had similar experiences with the passing of many more people, which made me less scared of death. My two younger brothers exited this world, only two years apart, before they were fifty. They were both good people with uniquely salient, endearing qualities in diverse ways. I mused on numerous occasions that I should have gone before them. Why not me?

More gripping among the stories that eased my trepidation about death is the story of an eight-year-old boy whom I got to know about through a friend. It was a story I never asked for, which has dramatically impacted my outlook on life and death.

Friendship and Love Underscored

Human Interactions: The Instructiveness of Life

Life is perhaps the best instructor we have; it offers us opportunities for knowledge, understanding, curiosity, wondering, growth, and amazement, all of these and more that sometimes even lead to our deeper incomprehensibility of it by nature of its sheer complexity, which, in turn, can open our eyes and minds wider as it unfolds. Life, just when you think you know it, something else highlights another angle, which can either make you a better or worse person, implying that life aggregates one's favorable and unfavorable experiences for an outcome, depending on how one responds to those experiences.

The most significant impact on our lives derives from our interactions with people. One of the many tools we employ to navigate life is relationships, within which friendships are validated or invalidated by individual experiences and responses. Co-occurring with love, friendship sounds and feels familiar; we can all claim that we know and have lived it; however, do we know its depth? Have we experienced it in all its flavors? Are there other experiences, first-hand or second-hand, that can widen and deepen our understanding of it? These and more are relevant questions that can allow us to ply the road of elevated understanding in friendship and similar relationships underscored by love.

Until recently, I thought I had copious knowledge of friendship. After all, I had experienced and lived it; I had seen it play out in other people's lives; I had learned that it could be esteemed or even purloined, and I thought I had witnessed it flourishing. At least that was the case until the late afternoon of January 2, 2024, a date that will forever be etched in my memory. It was the day when I observed a higher-order friendship. In this Goethe-like mode, "More light! More light," a phrase attributed to Wolfgang von Goethe, a German polymath and writer, I embraced the "light" for growth.

An Opportunity to Learn

It was a moment of unexpected connection. I had just finished some work on my laptop and felt the urge to take a brain break. I reached for my phone to check new messages and saw a few, among which were two audio messages. I rarely check audio messages, but the urge was irresistible that day. Before any aversion could kick in, I had pressed the play button. A resonant voice tempered by gratitude, joy, appreciation, and other similarly sanguine emotions uncommonly began to waft through my phone, filling me with an overpowering fervor of human connectedness. Although I heard little of what was said, I felt most of what I heard deep down to my essence, which was an outpouring of raw emotions, smacking joy, and relief. In a flash, considering that my reaction to the audio might have been hasty and knee jerked, I forwarded the audio to a friend, at least to evaluate if someone else would feel the weighty humanity I had felt while playing back the audio. Within minutes, my friend responded with the question: "What is this?" clearly not in a way to besmirch the audio message but only in a way to make sense of it. The fact that my friend, too, was deeply moved by the audio message was a powerful reminder of the universality of the emotions it evoked.

Mired in his puzzlement and mine, I quickly responded that it might have been a message about friendship and that I would call my friend (who had sent the audio) in the morning to get more details. I could tell my friend was as desirous as I was to get more context about the message. The context, however, came sooner than I had expected. My friend in Canada, who had forwarded the audio message to me, called in a matter of minutes and asked if I had played back the audio and knew what was happening. I told him I would need some gaps to be filled for comprehensibility. Intrigued by the story himself, he plunged right away into it.

Baby Ayodeji: The Light!

According to my friend, as evidenced and chronicled in the shared audio, a baby boy was born to a young couple, Aziza and Jinmi, on December 29, 2024, at Santa Monica Hospital in California. Elated as most fathers are when holding their newborn for the first time, Jinmi, the baby's father, marveled at the moment and beyond in a litany of emotions. He then shared his bubbling joy with his mother in an audio message later shared with others, including me. Self-narrating in the message, Jinmi's torrents of deep and graceful emotions were evident. He remarked that "today" was the happiest day of his life, a day he had been waiting for and one that would make him whole again, for he had been incomplete for twenty-six of his 33 years on Earth. He went on to say that "today," he finally got the blessing to name his prime progeny "Ayodeji," a name that packs the weight of grace, a two-fold bundle of joy, an overflowing and infinite recess of liveliness, and a name that would constantly invoke, according to Jinmi, the spirit or essence of his best friend, Ayodeji, who passed away 26 years ago and left a hole in Jinmi's being with his egress, a hole that had gaped each year since Ayodeji's exit and one that could now be patched with the birth and naming of his son "Ayodeji." As disclosed by my friend, Jinmi's audio message had been shared with the mother of Jinmi's deceased best friend, Ayodeji, glaringly in a tribute to his essence. The depth of Jinmi's emotions was a powerful testament to the intensity of love and friendship.

Ayodeji – Love and Friendship Robustly Personified

In her utterances in response to Jinmi's fawning over her son's brief but luminous life, Ayodeji's mother (26 years later) was utterly drowned in appreciative and appreciable ardor that anyone at all would 26 years later remember her transitioned son in the terms gracefully expressed by Jinmi, a childhood friend only six years old when Ayodeji passed. These are 26 years of friendship brought forward, not buried in the past. These are almost three decades of friendship sustained by love and unfleeting memories in the friend's absence. Often, when the leading player in a play leaves the play, it is the end of the show. Not in this case! Ayodeji plays on in Jinmi's life! This transcendence is the angle of fascination for me. I had good friends who passed away years ago, and I do not remember them faithfully enough, nor do I channel their influence relentlessly, as Jinmi does in the case of Ayodeji. I even had friends, at least four of them, who went on to the other side in the last two years, whose friendship I cherished while they were here, and now is rarely remembered by me. Who is this young man, Jinmi, who would recognize and dignify his childhood friend who passed away when he was just six years old? What was the relationship like? What were the exemplars of the friendship? The questions never ceased — what? why? and how? Submitting to the onslaught of these questions, I woke up at 2 am and messaged my friend that I had the forceful urge to meet with Jinmi to ask him these emerging and pressing questions. "Could you please get me his phone number?" I asked. Within hours, my friend in Canada got me Jinmi's phone number in Los Angeles. I called him, introduced myself, and offered my congratulations. We agreed to meet the next day in Santa Monica, about a 40-minute drive from his place and at least an hour from mine.

The Pride of Parenthood – Baby Ayodeji, Mom, and Dad

The Interface

The day was dour and nippy. Weather-wise, it was atypical for the perpetually sunny Los Angeles. The day required warm clothing, including scarves, jackets, and similar clothing. Jinmi appeared padded in a black winter jacket and a beanie hat. But he did not come alone; there were Aziza, Jinmi's wife, and baby Ayodeji, the newborn, padded up in his walker and intermittently baby-shrilling, the only way a newborn knows to communicate. Noticing my concern about Ayodeji's shrilling, Jinmi disclosed that Ayodeji had just been circumcised the day before and more than likely was in pain. According to Jinmi, however, they wanted me to see him in defiance of the pain. I thanked both parents for bringing him and for honoring me with his newness and presence.

Without delay, Jinmi launched into his narrative about Ayodeji, the deceased childhood friend after whom baby Ayodeji was named. Speaking glibly with perceptible candor, Jinmi described Ayodeji as his best friend and the most influential person (with the most imprint) in his life. Per Jinmi's reflection, Ayodeji was a friend and today remains his best friend even long after his demise. He was a full-fledged agent of humanity at seven years old. According to Jinmi, there were things in Ayodeji that were unseen in others, including adults. It was not only what he said but also how he said it. It was not only what he did but how he did it. His interactions with people were almost seamless and flawless. He loved freely and never pulled back, even when people did not return his love. He was radiant where others were unsmiling and presented with calmness, where everyone else was ruffled. He saw and spoke sense when and where other people lost reason, all with a faultless demeanor. Jinmi recalled that he and Ayodeji would binge-watch "Aladdin" on television in his room, passing comments and sharing emotions and moments of joy as they did. Even during play, Ayodeji was graceful, and there was always that opportunity to learn something from him.

As observed by Jinmi, there were many moments of marvel and no blemishes. Ayodeji, only a year older than Jinmi, was a role model of significant impact at eight years old. Of fantastic fascination for me is that Jinmi could notice all these benign attributes exemplified by Ayodeji, even now allowing such to bind and guide his life.

As remarked by Jinmi, Ayodeji's radiance was more widespread than anyone could tell. Among teachers at school, he was seen because he stood out. With the parents of his peers and church people, he was the quintessential child. In the community, he was the child everybody wished was theirs, precocious, unmalicious, and harmlessly mirthful. On the day Ayodeji died, following a bout with a life-threatening disease, the school was somber, the community was overwrought with the eeriness of loss, and friends like Jinmi were crushed by his death. It was a short stay for Ayodeji and a long-term loss for everyone else, more so for Jinmi. According to Jinmi, Ayodeji was often sick and was frequently taken away for treatment. To everyone, it was predictable that he would return as he had done on previous trips. Yes, he came back on his last trip, but not alive. Never to be seen again, never to be heard again, never to be touched again, but only to be felt in his robust essence, his raptured imprint imbibed and embodied by Jinmi and now baby Ayodeji, the newborn.

The Pride of Parenthood – Baby Ayodeji, Mom, and Dad

Congruent with Jimmi's view of Ayodeji is what the mom (Ayodeji's mom) feels about her son. Ayodeji endeared himself to all beyond his age bracket. He was cross-age radiant and even had a general in the army as his friend, the mom remarked. Mom further reminisced that Ayodeji was the nexus and the anchor of the friendship between Jinmi and one other friend. When Ayodeji ceased, the relationship between Jinmi and his other friend collapsed. For many years, according to Ayodeji's mom, Ayodeji's older brother, Babajide, became uncharacteristically reclusive and deflated because of his younger brother's death. It was only recently, just two months ago, that he came out of his long-term anguish dealing with his brother's death, having been told that Jinmi had named his son after his departed brother. In a high sense, Ayodeji continues to transmit good nature and humaneness, even in his wispy form. In and with his departure, he is here, never gone!

Jinmi today underscores love, unabrogated love, in his friendship with Ayodeji. "Ayodeji taught and showed me love," Jinmi gratefully said. Although Jinmi had been shown love by other people, especially his family constituents, he noticed that Ayodeji's brand was pure and blissfully rich. It was not the kind that struggled for attention only to please itself. It was simply angelic. Illustrating that love, courtesy of Ayodeji, in his life today, Jinmi says that he does not give love to get love; he only gives it and does not expect anything back, including love itself. The grace to show love is good enough for Jinmi, for in showing that love, he is whole and feels no vulnerability. He is complete with love, and his conscience is venerated.

I must confess that this kind of love is unexemplified by me at this point in my life. I give love and expect at least a modicum of it back; this is reciprocity, which, in turn, we all think nourishes emotional vibrancy and relationships. I have always argued that our world today is a show-me and show-off world, where we want to be seen and acknowledged for what we do, what we say, and what we give, including love, and where we disregard reason to garner self-centered adulation. Is this right, though? Is it worthy of probity? Yes! In the sphere of learning and growing, curiosity is worth a lot. Hence, I was willing to think deeper and more analytically about Jinmi's thoughts and practice of love. More than ever, I began to

The Pride of Parenthood – Baby Ayodeji, Mom, and Dad

think about how helpful and powerful it could be if one gave love without expecting it in kind from another person, quite daunting and taxing! However, yielding to that urge or nudge for open-mindedness, I ungrudgingly decided to give reason a chance, anchoring myself in how Jinmi made it thinkable and sensible with the examples he showed in his professional and personal orbits.

Jinmi and the Author

Jinmi co-owns an oil and gas company in Lagos, Nigeria, and at 33, is prosperous, something he continually appreciatively attributes to his late eight-year-old friend Ayodeji, all premised on the love shown him by Ayodeji. Jinmi revealed that not too long ago, his partner's and his management styles were disparate and almost demoralized their employees. According to Jinmi, his partner was high-handed, and he (Jinmi) was mindful of the sensibilities and psychological well-being of the employees. Where his partner's style was brutish, bullish, and aggressive, Jinmi's was subtle, assuaging, and more appealing to human decency. According to Jinmi, the love he shows his employees has yielded higher productivity, easier interactions, greater trust, and a workplace environment that nurtures growth and care, where every worker belongs and feels ownership in the company's successes and challenges. Where apprehension festers and threats consume the psyche, love becomes intensely undignified and sadly dissipates. However, in the case of Jinmi, especially with his brand of love, humanity is dignified plurally and collectively. Now a convert, according to Jinmi, his partner appreciates the propagation of love and human dignity in their company, born out of the accrued benefits. As a testament to Jinmi's standing with his employees and the public at large, hundreds attended his son's naming ceremony via Zoom recently, a sizable number of them corporate giants and stalwarts who may have been beneficiaries of Jinmi's incontrovertible love.

In his relationships with others, especially his wife, Jinmi has seen the multiple benefits of his selfless love. Speaking about his wife, whom he sees as a match in terms of unfettered love, Jinmi marvels that his 28-year-old wife is exceptionally generous with her love within her expansive family, resolutely steeping, farming, and firming everyone in that love, including older family members who now see her as the best gift the family has ever had for others. According to Jinmi, his wife Aziza is courteous and comely, never wanting to deal in spurious affront or misanthropic engagement with anyone. Her mantra and practice spell humility and grace when and where others conveniently see her decency as abject stupidity. She rises above follies beyond her age and is adored by most. Jinmi ascribes all of these to an absence of apprehension or insecurity in giving love and, in other words, giving it all on one's side and zeroing out on the other side because love rewards itself and is not dependent on the cognizance of the beneficiary, meaning that when one fixes their side, the other side is assured.

Jinmi would divulge that his wife has been a tremendous source of strength, vitality, and virility in maintaining the love inspired by Ayodeji. According to Jinmi, Aziza, for example, knows everything about Ayodeji and has allowed him to process and practice Ayodeji's love in enriching other people's lives, including their new baby's life. Jinmi lauds his wife's understanding and accommodation for allowing him to soldier on through the painful loss of his friend, something he refers to as his "baggage" in their relationship. For example, there was no contest when it came to their decision to name their newborn baby Ayodeji because Aziza had been told by Jinmi sustainably that Ayodeji would always be a significant influence in his life because he (Ayodeji) had taught him how to love, a thing that Aziza and others are greatly reaping from today. Extending this, Jinmi uninhibitedly thinks that Aziza, his wife, is a beneficiary (cumulatively) of all his relationships with the people in his life, including relationships with previous girlfriends. Looking at

his wife, Jinmi remarked, "I tell my wife that I am a product of all

the relationships I had with my girlfriends, good or bad, for each

relationship allowed me to grow and be a better person, a better

person that she is enjoying today. I think the same thing is true for

her." This is not too far-fetched in the scope of rationality in the

sense that an example and a non-example are reciprocally defining.

Growth, tied to love, lulls when adversity is absent in our

experiences and interactions with others. By the same token, when

love is not premised on reciprocity, it defeats malice, hate,

disappointment, and hatred; it defines and guarantees bliss and is

never "baggaged." Herein lies the power, the virtue, and the ultimate

reward of love, which maximally manifests in giving it, not

necessarily receiving it.

Surrogating now for Ayodeji, Jinmi's childhood friend, who taught

and imbued him with love, is baby Ayodeji, Jinmi's newborn. "We

had no best man at my wedding because Ayodeji could have been the

one. We left that role unfilled because of that," Jinmi reflectively

remarked.

In dealing with the kind of love he learned from his deceased seven-year-old friend, Ayodeji, Jinmi now feels the most fulfilling satisfaction of being ethereal, which is non-material! I join them and their new son in healing the world with this brand of uninhibited love. In a world subsumed or consumed by an exchange mentality (If I do not get it, I do not give it mental schema), we risk walking away from humanity.

A Personal Experience

Somehow, thinking about Jinmi's espousal regarding love, I remembered that I had once benefited from a similar experience that may never have registered had I not encountered Jinmi. On a road trip between Accra and Lagos years ago, I had a chance encounter with a man whose act of love and generosity remains quite memorable for me, perhaps not as weighty as the kind of love Jinmi learned from his deceased seven-year-old friend, but equally instructive.

In the border town of Sieme (Benin Republic), notoriously known for ruthless hustle, constant harassment, and brutal harangue of travelers, I was a victim of the context, trapped in the ever-consuming maleficence of the locale, including customs' exploitation, immigration extortion, and pedestrian swindling. The entire milieu was that of magnified chaos and heightened madness. Mentally and physically crushed by the dilemma, I felt that anywhere else in the world at the time would have been much preferable to this cesspool of zany exploits.

At 6 pm, it was getting darker, and I had been in the row for three hours, only covering a space of fifty yards, because every three yards of movement was a stop for unjustifiably taking money from us road trippers. It was designed to stretch time and distance, create intense frustration for travelers, and purposefully force money out of our pockets. After three grueling hours or more, I was ready to go but had another problem: my cell phone battery was completely dead, and I had no charger. My phone was the only way I had to communicate with my friends in Nigeria, as they had been worried that I might be in harm's way while traveling at night. I was scared, too, and had all kinds of dark imaginations about what could happen —robbery, kidnapping, or even death at the hands of miscreants.

I had to get a charger! Worried that my car could be vandalized or stolen if I stepped away from it, I decided it would be better to send one of the many people who readily and simultaneously volunteered to help me buy a charger. As I was about to hand money to one of them, out stepped a frail-looking man with a cell phone battery exactly like mine. "Here, take this! This is my battery. You can take it. Please do not give them money; they will not return, and it is getting dark. You must get to Lagos, and you need your phone," he said with a Christ-like certitude. I did not know what to say for a moment, and my eyes were transfixed on him. "Take it," he said again. "Well, thank you. Let me at least pay you for your battery," I said. "Please, no," he said gently but emphatically. I knew he would be offended if I pressed further, so I stopped. With my eyes lingering on him, I wondered why anyone would do this so compassionately and selflessly, in this case, without any forethought. His voice came back! "You have to go," he said, stressing that foreboding urgency again. I God-blessed him and got in my car. He sent me off with a smile and a prayer. For the rest of the trip, I had a place for him in my head and my heart.

I had to use the phone many times before I got to Lagos. It was his cell phone battery that got me through. He saw what I did not see, knew what I did not know, and averted harm for me at his own expense without any previous relationship between us. He asked for nothing, and when offered something for his act of kindness, he rejected it, only to self-generate his reward within himself, intrinsically! I opine herein that this is the most delightful reward, the most pleasant extension of self to others, and the crest of humanity.

Going back to Accra a week later, on the same road and at the same place, and going through the same extortionist maze, I heard a weak, quivering voice and looked in its direction. I saw a man with sunken eyes and a withering body. "Welcome, Sir! You made it back," he said with a stressed smile. The tone of familiarity suddenly registered in my head. He was the man who had given me his cell phone battery the week before. I apologized for not recognizing him instantly. He said it was okay, and I should not feel bad about it. Another man idling in the flank jumped into our conversation and then disclosed that my guy, the frail man, had been sick for months and that his condition was rapidly deteriorating. My conscience and compassion kicked in, and I pulled out a wad of cash to give him. He waved it off and refused to take it! He said he did not help me to get anything back from me; he did it to show me love. "That was all I had," he said. His gaunt face and desolate body were no match for his lucent gratification—subtle, pure, and hallmarking humanity. Although he did not say it, he left me with the task or challenge to treat people with the kind of love that does not presume, which is not predicated on anything but the dignity and decency of humanity.

The uncommon approach, which is generalizable as exemplified by the deceased Ayodeji, Jinmi, his wife, my friend in Sieme, and many icons and faceless people worldwide, is to indulge in that agape love. If all else fails, love stands and suffuses! While this may sound banal, love is the only thing that can evidence our collective achievement and triumph, regardless of our color, creed, intellect, and wealth. I am renewed, refreshed, and ready to walk the path of unconstrained love as taught by Ayodeji (Jinmi's deceased friend), as embraced and now practiced by Jinmi and his wife, and as affirmed by many unknown people worldwide. We all can be that link to and for that unfettered love. Baby Ayodeji, Jinmi's son, named after his deceased friend, is the newest link that Jinmi and his wife promise to nurture to serve love to others. This is a story I relish for its merits, more so in its offering of growth opportunities for you and me.

As I was processing the deaths of my great-grandfather, grandfather, aunt, Lance, and Ayodeji, death became increasingly softened and was easier for me to accept, as I was less frightened by its unfairness, mercilessness, and unpredictability. It is so now with me.

I am ready for the worst-case scenario, although I do not pray for it,

and I am not giving up. Indeed, accepting this bitter reality has

strengthened my will to heal and face the future, whatever it brings.

Surgery

As the surgery date got closer, I became more determined to live, but also to accept the possibility of not surviving the surgery. After all, death was the wielder of power in this case, as it does daily. It could be anywhere at any time without any reverence for any circumstances.

On the morning of the surgery, I was up earlier than usual, and so was my wife, who had the same apprehension as I did that our hope could elude us. If she was apprehensive, she did not show it, as she was busy getting things ready and reminding me of the pre-surgery instructions. I had been placed on diet restrictions three days before surgery, no solids and the usual, everyday foods, only clear liquids. It was difficult, but I took it one day at a time. Day one was the most difficult of the three days, as I craved every food I saw or smelled. Foods that ordinarily would not stoke my craving became imposing, mainly because of my wife's passion for cooking. She delights in cooking and making various dishes available at the same time. At the end of day one, I was more enduring and felt less tortured. Day two brought me closer to the finish line, and day three closed out my torturous fasting process, with the surgery as the next thing to worry about. The day finally came.

While waiting for our set-out time to leave the house for the surgical center, we were, independent of each other, trying to normalize our conversation. Still, it was clear that the day was not a typical day. The conversation was halting and choppy, as we tried to mask our fear that something could go wrong. I knew she was worried, and I tried my hardest to steer her away from her worries by attempting to lighten the situation. I told her that after my surgery, I would eat three home-cooked dishes simultaneously without leaving any leftovers. She pleasantly affirmed my desire and said she looked forward to my gaining back the weight I had lost.

As we left the house, I stopped at the door and looked around in the living room, wondering if I would ever see or be in it again. I thought about what my daughter would think and feel while she was away at school. Would Dad be okay? Would I see him again? Would he be the same person again? These were some of the questions I thought my daughter would be pondering. As a child, when my mom

Surgery

was seriously ill, I asked myself related questions while in a desolate

state. I had a feeling that it must have been tough for her.

On our ride to the hospital, the things along the way caught my

attention where they usually wouldn't—the trees, the sky, the cars,

the people, and more—because everything was outstanding and

gorgeous, blissful and almost heavenly. I remember thinking that if I

did not see this beautiful morning again, I would not forget the awe

of it. It was like an antidote against fear and an inducer of serenity.

Regarding surgery, I felt there was nothing to fear because I would

not be aware of the procedure itself, courtesy of anesthesia. I would

not be present in the moment and could only be aware of my being if

I were able to come back from surgery.

For the first thirty minutes at the surgery center, we went through the

check-in process, comprising identification, questioning, and

documentation signing. I was still in a state of calm. Following

identification and document signing, we were taken to an intake

room where a very friendly nurse directed that I do certain things to

get ready, including removing my clothes, donning a hospital

garment, and answering questions about my daily medications.

When she finished her part of the pre-surgery process, she said the surgeon would see me for more instructions and clarifications.

Minutes later, the surgeon, Dr. Kim, explained the procedure to us. My wife and I had no questions and were ready for the next step. A young man would soon come in with a gurney to take me for more preparatory work, including pre-anesthesia checks. As I was being wheeled off with my wife in tow, the wall art pieces in the hallway caught my attention and, for a moment, I was lost in the space of colors, designs, patterns, and aesthetics, which has always been a home, a place of fascination, for me. In this space, everything was secondary, even the surgery.

The surgery team informed us that the surgery room would be the next stop. As the nurses and others did the anesthesia precheck, I was alert and mindful of everything around me. There were checks and rechecks for documentation and my medication profile. There were also blood pressure and insulin checks. It was one of the rechecks that, for the first time in my life, revealed that I had a low blood sugar of fifty-nine. This was a significant discovery as it could have led to complications during the surgery. It was the anesthesiologist who ordered that my blood sugar be checked. Otherwise, they would have rolled me out without checking my blood sugar.

The anesthesiologist, a woman in her late forties or early fifties, came in with professionalism and readiness to check and recheck everything. She was forthright when asking me questions and meticulous in reading the documents handed to her. She asked the rest of the crew questions before okaying me for surgery. "See you shortly in surgery," she said and left. The rollout began five minutes later. As I was being rolled out, the crew told my wife that she would have to be in the waiting room as required by the surgical center regulations. Suddenly, I was alone and dejected by this necessary separation. The emotional toll of this separation was significant. Still, we had to endure, masking the sadness with hope that we would see again on the other side of surgery. I waved to her as she lingered, and she waved back. It was difficult.

Back in the hallway, I again saw those wall art pieces of colorful landscapes and geometric shapes. Within seconds, it occurred to me that the dominant element in all the pieces was nature, including the sky, hills, flowers, geometric shapes, and more, all metaphoric for nature, which never fails to bring me bliss. Sedated by calmness, I was delivered to the surgery room. A moment later, I was placed on the surgical table with white robotic arms overhead. I saw the masked faces of the anesthesiologist and surgeons. I heard and felt air from a plastic mask over my mouth and nose. The air was the last thing I heard and felt. Darkness! If asked today where I was while I was in surgery, I would draw a blank, as I had no awareness of my being. Was that a short-term death?

Recovery

I was told that my consciousness returned about four hours later. The room was not anything like the surgery room. There were no robots and imposing equipment, no anesthesiologists, nor was there the surgeon, Dr. Kim. There was only an attending nurse, who told me that surgery was over and that I would remain in the room for two to three hours for observation before I would be moved to the regular hospital room. I marveled at the first sight of daylight again through the hospital window. I heard voices in the hallway, smelled the medicated air in the room, touched my stomach, felt the stitches, and, of course, tasted the blandness of my saliva. I was back and considered myself lucky. It was like a rebirth.

I felt very good-natured towards everyone and everything. As the nurses were coming in to do their follow-up checks, I met them with smiles and light banter. They similarly responded and asked how I was feeling. "Pained, but okay," I answered. I was weak but sustained by hope and optimism brought about by my coming out on the other side of surgery alive. Suddenly, everything that was once a problem or challenge for me was no longer a threat, and I settled into this wonderful equilibrium of inner peace. Every moment was special, as I no longer saw my worries as threatening; I saw them as an opportunity to live and triumph, even when the outcome fell short of my expectations.

One of the nurses was particularly pleasant in that she spent time with me asking questions, perhaps to know my story. She genially presented herself and was soothingly matronly. Following up on all my responses to her questions, she made positive comments and was confident that I would be better and stronger with time and a determined and cheerful outlook on life. She gave me more than medications and the usual services; she appealed to the deepest side of me, the emotional side of me, to strengthen my whole being. She undoubtedly increased the value of who I was in the few minutes she was with me. She allowed me to see and feel the empathetic side of relationships, short or long-term. Before the experience with this nurse, I had been contending with seeing the good side of things in everything, even when it was blighted. However, I was struggling until I had this reawakening experience with the nurse. There and then, I recommitted to nurturing and sustaining a benign attitude to life. It has made my life easier.

About two hours into my recovery in the recovery room, it was time for me to be moved to a regular hospital room. Although I was still in pain, the mover softened my pain with his witty chats and jokes. "You'll get over this and be your naughty self again, eating what is not right for you, thinking you are Superman, and weakening your resolve with doubts. It happens to most of us. I was a naughty boy once. Do not be like me," he counseled. In his unseriousness, he was serious. He had a message for me that was bundled in humor and delivered with candor.

Once in my hospital room, life slowly came back beyond the hospital. I started thinking about my life in successive flashes, from childhood and adolescence through the present and into the future. What would I do from here on? How would I allow myself to learn as much as I could? What would I do to aid the lives of others, and what would I do to develop my inner peace and contentment? Each of these questions prompted relevant flashbacks to my childhood and adolescence, the good influences of family, friends, and people from whom I have immensely benefited. Then I began to see a pattern of transcendent humanity for which I should strive, as this is the only thing that could give meaning and relevance to my life. But first, I must work on myself to realize this objective.

My wife came back to the hospital following a few hours of rest at home while I was sleeping. It was glaring that she saw that being able to chat with me post-surgery was a gift of time and meaning. We both sat next to each other and launched into talks about us, with daylight coming through the huge window in the room, symbolically allowing us to think and see beyond the room to avail ourselves of the future. It was sanguinary, to say the least.

The future was back in the picture, and I could not wait to embark on it with God in the saddle. After all, being afforded another chance was not my doing. Imbued with optimism and a renewed sense of being, I was eager to go home and be with my wife and daughter, away from the somberness of the hospital. The surgeon had assured me that barring complications, I could be discharged the next day after surgery. At 3 pm the next day, I was still in my hospital room waiting to be released. I thought everything had gone well according to the standards set by the surgeon, especially the results of the many tests conducted. Beyond the surgeon's call based on test results, I considered myself fit enough to go home. I could stand, walk, and speak clearly. I was ready to be in that place of comfort called home. By 4 pm, we were still waiting, and it became increasingly doubtful if I would be discharged that day. For a long time, there were no hospital workers in sight, and we became worried that the surgeon might have seen something that would make them keep me hospitalized.

Dejection began to swell as frustration snowballed. My wife paced the room intermittently, silently praying that the crew would show up and release us. Our conversations dried up because my discharge on this day seemed threatened. Patience became a thing to adopt, as time could not catch up with my wish. The wait continued, and I quickly plunged back into the future to escape the slowness of the present. I reverted to self and started thinking about what I could do to be a better person henceforth, mainly to dignify the new lease on life I had been granted. Urgency came to mind, not in the vein of haste but in the mode of being deliberate and prompt, similar to an aversion to taking things for granted. I realized that I had been habitually tentative with things, including daily, basic things, and had minimized my potential. Even now, as I write, I'm thinking of many things: books and articles I could have finished and published, investment documents written years ago waiting to see the light of day, and many more things that I could have pursued that I left dormant even when I had time. Time! I started ruminating about time.

Time and Its Urgency

Time is an independent entity operating without regard for anything, innocently unsentimental and unbiased. It has a longer life than any of us and can cease for anyone while living on for itself. None of us has an infinite amount of it, hence urgency matters.

Before surgery, nothing had bothered me more than my tendency to linger unnecessarily. I had wanted to do something about it because I had seen the deficits in my life mounting. I was tentatively committed to changing and struggled because I did not take time seriously or value time then. It was my diagnosis of cancer that roused a deeper understanding of time in me as it relates to urgency. There and then at the hospital, in a silent prayer and willful candor, I recommitted to treating my actions with urgency, as I might not have the time I thought I had, that tomorrow and the next moment might not be real. I felt awakened, renewed, and ready to make this resolve central to my being.

A nurse with a familiar face who had been to my room more than ten times earlier in the day walked in. She had a folder in her hands with some documents in it. "Before we discharge you, there are certain things I would have to do," she said while rifling through the papers. She showed me one of the documents and said, "These are the dos and don'ts after surgery. Next, this is for your medications." She went on, demanding my signature where necessary as she went through everything, document by document. A wave of relief and joy washed over me. I was sure I would be released in the next hour or less. It was clear I was being discharged, another thing to reaffirm my being back. I signed the last document, and the nurse asked if we had any questions. We did not. She handed two bags of my belongings to my wife. The nurse wished me well and exited the room. Smiles and relief set in. I changed clothes and was wheeled to the curbside minutes later while my wife went to get the car.

While waiting for the car to arrive, I looked pensively into the horizon and saw a cascading future, even as I remained present in my immediate surroundings. I could see cars dropping off or picking up patients, the dimming daylight morphing into simmering dusk, the clatter of gurneys being loaded onto and off ambulances, and the chatter of passers-by as they went in and out of the hospital. To them, I said hello, and they responded genially. The hospital, the nexus of health or ill health, was the connecting point. We all were there and bound by the same dilemma, which, I presumed, increased the level of our humanity. I felt a profound sense of peace and gratitude, and was worry-free, knowing we were all bound by the same plight.

As I reveled in the moment's tranquility, the car rolled in, and it was time to go home, finally! My wife assisted me in getting into the car, and off we rolled. Just as it was the day we went in for surgery, everything along the route home mattered to me and my life, the people, the trees, the cars, the sky, the Sun, and more. I saw everything, of which I was just a tiny part. I thought there was no way I could fully exist without deference to those elements around me that could determine my humanity. I realized nature was a big part of it, mixed in with the human dynamics resulting from human interactions and activities. I mused that I could not ignore these things as they must be deliberately planted into my life and growth, all with appreciation and a sense of harmlessness in my interaction with nature and the people in my space or orbit. I considered this as I trudged into the house with my wife. Thirty-two hours after surgery, the tenets for my reset were shaping up, and I was glad that my health dilemma was now the basis for my refreshed being, part of a larger whole.

Recovery at Home

We got home, and it felt like home, an insulated, private space for me to heal physically and emotionally, a niche of psychological safety. My wife had prepared everything from liquid foods to necessary hospital supplies, including smaller items I had not even considered. She seamlessly transitioned into the role of spouse and caregiver when we returned home. "How are you feeling? "Pele" (Sorry in Yoruba, my language). You need to eat something. Let me make you something special that is liquid. You will love it. You have lost weight, and we need to get it back. You will have to drink a lot of water, you know. We must make sure that we do everything as advised at the hospital. Let us check the hospital discharge instructions for all we must do," she said, speaking to herself and me. She was cognitively reminding herself of the tasks she needed to complete to help me recover. Her dedication to my recovery was unwavering.

I know her; she can be very intense to the point of obsession and relentlessness. Helen, my wife, knows a lot more than people assume. She cares more than anyone can ever guess. You will not see the depth and extent of her care and empathy unless you get close to her. She is compulsive about hygiene and health, often repulsed by bacteria and viruses. Her sense of smell is so keen that she can catch a whiff of anything in the air that most people cannot, all with her diminutive nostrils. My nostrils are bigger but less adept at detecting foul and clean air than hers. When she says something is foul in the air, you'd better believe it. I have lost all the bets on smell detection with her.

Helen has reasons to safeguard when it comes to health and hygiene. She is an easier target for bacteria and viruses, by her admission. She tries to avoid using public toilets because of her high susceptibility to infection, and, at home, the toilets must constantly be cleaned and disinfected. She is "drivenly" curious about health, too. She reads about health issues and watches endless hours of documentaries on anything related to well-being and wellness. Doubtlessly, she knows more than I do in the health domain, and I know not to quibble with her wellness knowledge. I have always thought that her self-satisfaction niche, a domain in which she can easily excel, is healthcare at a higher level. She cares and loves care.

In the heat of COVID in 2020, I benefited from Helen's passion and giftedness for care. I had just returned from a trip to Africa and was in good spirits to hit the ground running with a host of things to finish, meetings to have, and people to see or be with. No sooner did I get home than I started unpacking, cleaning the house, and doing things the way I wanted them done, just done! Following chores at home, I drove out at dusk to reflect on my trip, as it might influence my future. This private engagement was illuminating, and, as a result, I was ready to tread on the clear path of my next pursuits. No doubt, I was in good spirits.

The next morning, something felt a bit awkward. I felt some lethargy and the onset of something unpleasant, as I was coughing at intervals and incrementally feeling feverish. I thought it was the usual touch-and-go flu, the type that Mucinex or DayQuill would sink, but it was not. The next day brought more fatigue, coughing, and fever. I became weaker and less productive in my thoughts and actions. My voice became weaker and increasingly hoarse, with my breath labored and shortened. Walking was taxing, eating was not appealing, and ordinarily simple activities were no longer simple. It was clear that something was wrong. I started to lose weight, looking gaunt, gutted, and physically depleted.

To make matters worse, I began to consume Gatorade for energy and to fill my empty stomach, recklessly ignoring my diabetic struggles. Something was wrong, and I did not want people to know and panic. In answering calls, I was deliberately tweaking my voice so as not to give my condition away. I also politely shortened the calls to conserve my energy for breathing. I did this for two days, and no one could detect my dilemma. However, 4,000 miles away, Helen had the suspicion of trouble. She called my sister, who was fifteen to twenty minutes away from me, and asked if I was okay. In her unrelenting way, she told my sister that she was sure I was undergoing some health challenges. She is stupendously prescient and can see, hear, smell, taste, and feel where others do not. She was right. I was not well. She sounded urgent to my sister and convinced her to check on me. My sister did and found out. The evening my sister came over was loaded with everything that gave me away, my lost weight, tiredness, extremely high blood sugar (in the high 400s), and high blood pressure, among other disastrous health issues I faced. My sister was shocked and worried that I had contracted COVID and that it was taking me down fast. She panicked and immediately took me to the nearest urgent care. On our way to the urgent care, she called her daughter and her husband, who are both health practitioners, and informed them of my condition.

At the urgent care, my awareness of my deteriorating state was more than my cognizance of the urgent care context. I was weak, worried, and just wanted to be in bed. The doctor saw me and asked COVID-related questions, all of which I answered yes to. Even I was sure that I had COVID, and this was around the time COVID was rife and unforgivingly virulent, dropping people mercilessly. I was afraid, to say the least, and my sister was, too.

The attending doctor ordered a COVID test, which was done right there at the urgent care facility. About an hour later, the doctor called me to review the results and embark on treatment. "Negative," she curtly said. "You don't have COVID," she remarked further. "What could it be then?" I asked. She explained that since the symptoms were like those of COVID-19, she would prescribe COVID-19 medications. She gave me the medicines and advised that I go to an emergency room should my condition worsen. Right about 10:30 pm, we got back home, and, at 11:30 pm, my niece and her husband showed up with medications and handy health paraphernalia such as breathing aides and glucose meters. They tested my blood sugar level, and it was still high. My breathing was stressed, and my oxygen level was very low. Just like the doctor did at the urgent care, they treated my condition as if it were COVID. Beyond the medications they gave me, however, they made sure I had steroids and breathing treatments. They had driven two and a half hours to take care of me and would stay another three hours for my condition to show signs of improvement. Yes, there were signs that things were getting slightly better for me. Within hours, my blood sugar dropped ten points, from 450 down to 440. My fever also came down a few points, and my oxygen level gained two points. For my sister, niece, and her husband, there was hope that I could get better incrementally if I stayed on the medications prescribed and sustained the recommended treatment. They went home a bit relieved.

I would not be here today without the trio's prompt and urgent response to my health crisis that night. There is no way I can separate Helen from this, though. She sounded the alarm. In her usual character, she sensed that something was anathema to my health and that I was covering it up.

My sister called Helen the next day to tell her that I was not as well as she had suspected. It turned out that Helen had started making travel arrangements to leave Accra for Los Angeles to see what was wrong with me and offer whatever support was necessary. She told my sister she was on her way to Los Angeles and called to inform me that she would be in LA the next day. When I tried to dissuade her, she rebuffed my reasoning and explained that it was too late for her to change plans, as she had already purchased her ticket and was going to the airport. Obviously aggrieved, she asked in a tone of disappointment, "Why didn't you tell me?" I had an answer for her, an explanation I was not ready to offer because it might sound silly, weak, insensitive, or arrogant. My response to the same question from my sister the day before had fallen flat and drawn a bit of ire and hurt from her. "I don't want to bother anyone," I said weakly. "You don't want to bother anyone? Who says it is a bother? It may be a bother to you, but to us it is not. She said in her typical, caustic but love-intentioned manner. "I'm okay," I said, trying again to minimize the severity of my condition to lessen her worries, but it did not work, as the truth was right there in front of her. I was there, weak and scarily emaciated in a ghostly way, hardly able to breathe through a simple sentence. "You're not okay! Look at yourself! You need prayers and care. Thinking you do not need anyone is not a virtue that wins. It isolates and destroys," my sister philosophically quipped. I kept quiet and could not refute her claim; it was irrefutable because, in my condition then, I was the perfect example of what she thought I was denying and hiding. I had my own rational reason for not wanting anyone to know what I was going through, though. I detested, and still hate, bothering people with my needs, always considering what sacrifices they would have to make to accommodate my needs. I sometimes feel for people more than I do for myself. Rather than depriving other people of something, I would rather deny myself —something that some people think is naively informed. As I stated elsewhere in this book, it was, and still is, a struggle for me, even though I knew my sister was not extreme in her remark about my attitude.

Back to the night of what I believe was a night of divine rescue, following the departure of my sister, niece, and my niece's husband, I started to feel psychologically better as the dawn loomed, maybe as a result of the compassion and support I had been accorded by people around me, mixed in with the knowledge that Helen was coming—perhaps evidence that support could be healing in many ways.

The next morning, I got up and was not destituted or defeated by my condition, although still physically weak. Helen had told me the day before that she would take an Uber home from the airport in consideration of my debilitated state. I could not drive and had not driven in a few days. However, I felt differently the morning Helen was to arrive. Boarded, seated, and ready to take off, Helen called from New York, and I told her that I was feeling better and would pick her up at the airport. She was on edge, but I insisted I could do it. The steroids and other medications I had taken kicked in and wildly boosted my energy.

On my way to the airport, I began thinking of ways to demonstrate my love and gratitude to Helen. Kissing her would be ordinary and out of place at the height of COVID-19, hugging would be pedestrian and not enough, and merely holding her hands would not be impressive. So, I thought of a more dramatic approach. I would go down on my knees and extend my hands of gratitude to her, and have someone capture the moment with a camera. I felt this would be a timeless example of my appreciation for her love and care. It was so beautiful in my head, but it did not happen as planned. In fact, it did not happen at all.

Helen was in the waiting area in front of the airport when I saw her. With my phone in my hand, I was ready to have someone capture my beautiful plan on camera. I walked towards a lady standing nearby and asked her to take a picture of Helen and me. What happened next was disappointing; the lady quickly sidestepped and moved away from me. She was uncomfortable with the request, and, maybe, scared. "Hey, what are you doing?" Helen asked, sounding confused by what was happening. I hugged her and thanked her for caring, loving, and giving. She asked me again what was happening with the lady, and I explained what I was trying to do to show my appreciation. She respectfully told me I did not have to be that dramatic. She reminded me that the lady's reaction was warranted because we were in the throes of COVID-19, which could provoke such a reaction from anyone. I noticed that she looked at me in a worrisome way, rather unusually. I knew she was unsettled by what she was seeing. Weeks later, she disclosed to me that she was also scared when she saw me at the airport, as I looked tense and frighteningly excited, even aggressive. My ghostly appearance, having lost a lot of weight, according to her, did not help. "Yombo, why didn't you tell me? You are not well. This is more serious than I thought. You have lost a lot of weight. Anyway, I am glad to be here. God is with us. You will be alright," she remarked with a note of confidence and trust in God, her usual optimistic affirmation.

Helen loves Asian cuisines, and, on our way home, we stopped to get takeout food from one of her favorite Asian restaurants. When we were ready to place our order, the cashier did not mind us. She had her back to us and would not respond when we repeatedly asked for the menu. When our eyes met, she appeared agitated and quickly disappeared. Helen would whisper in my ear that I had scared the woman with my brusque approach and frightening look. I was unaware of all of this until I was cautioned and informed by Helen about how people were reacting to me. I suspected that my intimidating posture was caused by the steroids I was on. Ordinarily, I was not like this; I was moderately courteous with people. I felt sad about this and have now become more mindful of my demeanor with people. My mantra now is that if you cannot spark joy and savoir-faire in people, do not contribute to their agonies. I have realized that one of the ways one can do this is to say hello to people with perceivable, genuine, and human compassion for the existence of others. It feels good to be an agent of humanity in our interactions with others. The awakening of this in me was no doubt intensified by how I had conducted myself with the two ladies who, on the same day, an hour apart, had felt disrespected, perhaps demeaned, by my behavior. It all felt like a sin against humanity, a misanthropic and self-hating attitude. It remains for me a road to not travel on.

When we got home from the restaurant, Helen was ready to do the tasks of a caregiver right on the heels of a 16-hour flight. Although the house was decently clean, Helen still cleaned and sanitized the bedrooms, bathrooms, kitchen, and other areas. She has always been hooked on cleanliness; hence, I was not surprised. It was also during COVID-19 when cleanliness was warranted more than ever.

After cleaning and checking the house to see what food items were available, she decided that we would have to go to the store, as most of the food items at home were unsuitable for me. According to her, the objective was to avoid sugar-laden, fatty, and unhealthy foods in general. She strongly suggested lots of vegetables and proteins to replenish what I had lost. We went to the store, where Helen took her time to check the health qualities of each item. I observed that prices and time (at the store) were not the concern for her. She took her time to ensure that everything she picked was what I needed. We filled the cart and headed home. I began to think less about my condition because grocery shopping with my spouse felt like a regular, high-frequency chore that married couples would do together. It was a welcome break from being alone and languishing in worries brought about by ill health. Her presence was a source of comfort and strength. I was deeply grateful for her unwavering support and care.

Each meal was fresh, healthy, rich, and filling. Helen filled the plate with assorted items each time, including vegetables and proteins. She intermittently reminded me to eat as much as possible for weight gain. It was different from when I was taking care of myself. Where I was basic, she was deluxe. I began to enjoy it. Every day, Helen would set aside some time in the morning to plan the meals for the entire day, breakfast, lunch, and dinner, along with snacks at intervals. She took this seriously and sometimes would be self-talking aloud while planning. Nothing was planned and prepared haphazardly; everything was thought through, indicating that she did not take this lightly. That was just food. There were other things.

On the night of her arrival, I told Helen to have a room for herself for fear that I might infect her with whatever I had. I was worried because it would be disastrous if we broke down simultaneously. She looked at me with a lingering gaze and said we would be okay. With that, we said good night to each other, and she went into one of the rooms. However, not quite an hour later, she was in my room. "Heck it! I am here to care for you and will be in this room with you. I want to know when you are in pain, when you need something, and even when you are okay. I feel more comfortable when I am where you are. I know what you are going to say. COVID-19? You do not have COVID. We will be alright," she said with no small conviction. I had no rebuttal for her. That also opened another window into her heart.

A few days into Helen's care of me, I saw that a pattern was looming. Each day began with breathing therapy. Helen would boil water and set up the paraphernalia for the treatment. She would direct and supervise the process and clean up when we were all done. The process lasted anywhere from 40 to 50 minutes and required me to inhale treated steam deeply for up to five minutes while covering up to trap the steam. Although seemingly simple, I noticed that the therapy could be challenging to endure. There were many times I almost quit the treatment, but Helen prevented this and urged me to see the process through each time. I was always drenched with sweat in bubbles, with moments of hard coughing to clear my breathing tracks. The steam was stinging on my skin, making it difficult to keep my head buried in the steaming bucket for as long as recommended. Helen was there, though, and encouraged me to invoke and sustain my willpower. After a few days of this therapy, my chest, olfactory tracts, and head began to clear. I could feel the improvement in my breathing, energy level, and mental acuity. The drugs, therapy, and, most especially, Helen's care were all working cumulatively. I was feeling better. I was lucky.

During the breathing therapy, Helen would take pictures to show me how I looked. I was glad she did because I would not have known the severity of my state without them (the pictures). They were grippingly scary. My face was sunken and looked hollow. My rib cage was skin-deprived and revealed its outline. Atop my frail body, my huge head delicately sat. I remember looking at the pictures and thinking I was far removed from humans but much closer to E.T. in Spielberg's masterpiece of the same name. It was scary. Helen still has the pictures and, occasionally, shows them to me —not to sadden me but to remind me of the power of the will or determination to live and the guts to rise above impediments. Today, these pictures have become a recurrent imagery of strength rather than surrender for me. They symbolize the synthesis of courage, care, empathy, dedication, and reasonable efforts to defeat adversity. This has been tremendously helpful in my latest bout with health challenges, and

Helen is a welcome fixture in it. No doubt, it is a spirit that I must sustain.

Recovery at home following surgery continued, and Helen was again in the center. She would make available whatever I wanted to eat if it was not in the way of my recovery. "Let me get you something nice and healthy to eat, " she would say. Sure enough, each meal was nice and healthy. Over the years, I have learned not to doubt her confidence in her cooking skills. She treats cooking like science and is passionate about it. It is something she enjoys doing. She is a foodie, an unrelentless gourmet. She particularly loves it when one raves about her food and finishes it. When she sees me humming and shaking my head from side to side while eating, she knows that the food sits well with me. "It is good, right? I am glad you love it. Healthy food makes good health. Eat all," she usually says. I ate all of it each time. I did not know where it came from, but I had this monstrous appetite during my recovery. Eating was one of the easiest things I did, and it brought me joy, hope, and energy.

In the early days of my recovery, we mostly stayed home except for when we had to go to the stores or when I had medical appointments.

Accompanying me to all my appointments, Helen drove, as driving was more demanding than what I could spare in energy and alertness. At the appointments, as a "health head," she asked questions and was able to talk expertly about my recovery patterns. As we struggled through recovery, each day was a day of intimacy and mutual affection for us. We were in a much smaller space, our own real and psychological space, shaped by my surgery and our recovery efforts. It brought us closer to each other in a cherishable way. It allowed us to share the moments with the resolve to triumph, and, at the same time, it opened the door to the future.

The responsibility of care is not an easy undertaking. It requires patience, empathy, commitment, and a passion of significance. This was exemplified again for me in my recovery after surgery, especially in direct care.

Helen got all the necessary things that I had not thought about. She was ahead of me in our readiness for recovery. Before the hospital released me, Helen, for example, had stocked the house with things we would need, many of which I had not thought we would need. For instance, she purchased loose cotton T-shirts and easy-to-wear sportswear pants. Her reasoning was that anything too tight and thick would make me uncomfortable. She bought many of these T-shirts and sports pants to ensure I had a change of fresh clothes daily, which was part of her good hygiene and cleanliness principle. She did laundry frequently, for she did not want dirty clothes in an ugly pile. Again, she believed that, and still does, that dirtiness would never fail to worsen an illness.

When I had my catheter on, Helen would empty and clean the container at intervals every day, doing everything meticulously and with steady hands. She did this more than five times a day and did not show any attitude of resentment. At intervals, she checked to see if the container had to be emptied. At times, I wondered how long she could keep this going. When I thanked her for all she was doing, she simply said it was her job. "This is what we are facing, and we have to be tough on it," she once remarked. Tending to the catheter went on for weeks, with instances of malfunction that warranted going back to the clinic or emergency room three times. However, Helen was consistent with her diligence and commitment through it all. Seeing how much work she was doing and the energy expended,

I felt guilty and tried to get her to do less, but she did not budge and kept piling on things she wanted to do to take care of me. She was unrelenting.

Daily bathing was another thing Helen took on. She insisted on bathing me daily for reasons she convincingly explained to me. According to her, cleanliness has a way of fast-tracking physical and psychological recovery. She explained further that an ailing body gives off the foulest odors and chases healing agents away. At the same time, a clean body hastens recovery. Frankly, I did not want to bathe because I had just had surgery and could still feel the soreness of my surgery spots. When I told her this, she told me not to worry, as we would find a way to get it done. I thought this would be a simple matter of wiping me down, but I was wrong.

Helen took upwards of 30 minutes daily to get the bathing paraphernalia ready. There were bathing gel, lotion, towels, bowls, plastic sheets, a sponge (yes, a sponge), and other items she assembled for each session. We could not use the bathroom for fear that I could fall because I was weak. We also did not want to get my surgery spots wet, a no-no, according to my discharge instructions.

Helen figured out that the bedroom, specifically the space on my side of the bed, was a better place. For one thing, I could sit on the bed and get sponged and wiped down, eliminating the risk of falling and making it convenient for her to reach all the necessary spots carefully. She was thorough but careful, taking her time to scrub, wipe, and lotion me up. I thought the process was tedious and overly demanding of both of us, more so her, as she was the one doing the work. I felt for her and, at times, suggested we skip the process. Still, she insisted that we must be consistent with the frequency, often reiterating her health and hygiene mantra that good hygiene expedites healing. This was confirmed for me on the first day that she bathed me. I felt clean and fresh right after bathing and was pleased mentally. It was an accomplishment, a much-desired milepost in my recovery. Although I detested doing it because it was arduous, bathing soon became a thing that hallmarked each day of my recovery, something I could measure my progress with. It was therapy in my recovery, courtesy of Helen.

Recovery for me was not as easy as I had thought. In fact, surgery was more bearable than recovery. It was completed in less than four hours, but recovery was a long haul with many challenges. After my

discharge, the first two weeks were quite episodic with brutal

discomfort resulting from excessive pain, mostly in my stomach and

around my surgical sites. Although Tylenol was recommended to

stem the pain, it was not strong enough to quell it. My stomach was

like a battlefield, filled with volleying artillery and erupting like a

volcano. I could hear and feel it all in my stomach and would scream

for mercy and relief. This could go on for half an hour each time, but

that half an hour seemed like an eternity. It was grossly tormenting.

When this happened, Helen would be there to comfort me, at times

holding my hands and uttering words of comfort. The rumbling in

my stomach triggered dreadful pain in the areas of incision that were

freshly stitched. It seemed like a big rock was in my stomach,

moving from side to side and top to bottom. While it happened, I

was in a state of distress, tormented both physically and mentally. I

kicked, yelled, grimaced, and uncharacteristically cursed

uncontrollably, struggling to find relief. Furthermore, in my efforts

to seek relief, often in confusion, I would move from place to place, usually between the bedroom and the living room, trying to stave off the pain, all in the early days of recovery.

I vividly remember what happened one night when my agonies were unbearably heightened. I was in bed and had managed to sleep through a brewing pain. And then it happened. I felt the jarring movement in my stomach, very eruptive and disturbing, with a lot of pain. It had never happened like this before, especially with this much virulence. It instantly overtook my state, space, physicality, and faculty. It was in total control. I winced, grimaced, and cringed. I even reacted with a muffled scream, as I did not want to wake Helen up. She had relentlessly cared for me earlier that day and must have been tired. Not to disturb her sleep, I struggled to get out of bed and lumbered to the living room, where I could react to the pain with my natural reflexes. In the living room, the rumbling persisted, and the pain was unyielding. It kept on, more torturous than it had been minutes before. I screamed, kicked, and did things randomly without any reasoning. I remember standing up, pacing back and forth, then sitting down and rocking from side to side within seconds. It was turbulent, to say the least. It was clear to me, even in that confused state, that I did not know what I was doing. I was drowned in massive pain.

Then, desperately seeking a diversion from the pain and in that random reaction, I picked up the remote control and turned the TV on. And there, on the screen, was the live coverage of Pope Francis' funeral. Instantly, I psychologically disconnected from my seething agonies and felt this empyrean calm. It seemed my interest, more specifically, my high regard and huge admiration for the Pope, had taken over the moment. Even before his demise, Pope Francis had always been a subject of fascination and inspiration for me. I saw him as a person bigger than any of us, while he saw himself as ordinary as all of us. In a moment of faith and spirituality, I subconsciously made a supplication to God out loud. "God, please let this pain go away. God, let this pain go away. God, let this pain go away," I said three times. Sure enough, in the vein of a divine intervention, the pain began to fizzle until it left my body. I watched the entire coverage, about four hours, to the end without anything unsuitably episodic. It was tranquil and healing. At 2:23 a.m., grateful for and surprised by this moment of bliss and elation, I quickly reached for my phone and started crafting a message to close friends with whom I could comfortably share my spirituality.

I wrote:

It is 2:23 a.m., and I am watching the funeral of Pope Francis, and my pain fizzles, not oozes, as it did 60 minutes before now. The pain opened the door to relief through Pope Francis, "faithwork!" Pope Francis was exceptional, which may be a burnishing reminder that life can be immortal, even in its breathless state. He was a stand-up person, error-prone, but never afraid to point out the fragility of his faith. Humility was his strength, and humanity was his passion. Now wispy but present, he speaks to us. It is blissful in this space and state. From here on, it is a value-added life. God is with us always! Thank you for sparking spirituality in my life—quite enriching! I am doing much better. Thank you. Thank God!

As the credits rolled on the screen, a gentle sleep sneaked in and took me "lands away." I woke up the next day feeling stronger and better.

My recommended diet was another thing that posed a challenge to me in my recovery, although not as troubling or traumatic as the pain. Before surgery, I was placed on plain liquids for four days and semi-liquid foods for four more days after surgery. The first four days were difficult, especially the first day, but Helen offered encouragement and an informed sense of diet. She tried each time to make the ordinary more appealing. Each liquid meal she had for me had something that made it special. The first day was difficult, but once I survived it, the rest of the days were easier. After surgery, we continued with liquids, and, at some point, Helen, drawing on her improvisation skills, gradually moved me to semi-solids until I was cleared for straight solids. The day I was cleared for straight solids was special for both of us in that Helen had been looking forward to making a variety of dishes for me, for she wanted me to gain all the weight I had lost as quickly as possible. "When the husband is unnecessarily lean and emaciated, it's a blemish on the wife," she sometimes quips. However, she means it. It is delightfully rewarding for her to feed people in her unique way.

Recovery – Gradual Release

As we continued in my recovery, I got stronger and could do some things by myself, unassisted. For example, we started bathing in the bathroom instead of the bedroom, with Helen gradually letting me do this independently. I was also motivated to be independent of her, as I saw that she was doing a lot in a day. As the stitched spots were healing and the pain was dissipating, I could do more, and this was uplifting for me in that it became a good measure of my progress. Getting in and out of the car was no longer painful; I could move freely and help myself in the kitchen with simple things like water or a cup of coffee. I could see traction, and Helen and I could feel it. The future was possible and within reach. We began to talk about the future more in good spirits, something inspired by my on-track recovery. I also thought about returning to work sooner than I had planned. I love to do and enjoy what I do. My job as an educator, combined with my private pursuits, is very fulfilling because it allows me to learn daily and see the benefits of human interactions. I often tell people that I have the best job in the world, being in the front row observing how the mind works and its capacity in different people and contexts. I wake up every day, often looking forward to new things I will find, hence the excitement to return to work sooner than planned. Then something unexpected happened that reversed the course of my excitement and recovery.

It was a beautiful Wednesday morning, approximately two weeks after my surgery, and I was ready for our pre-planned things to do that day. Among other things, Helen and I had planned to go downtown to get some food items for the special dishes she had promised me. I was in good spirits and began the day with light banter, flaunting my sense of humor with my wife and daughter. I was thrilled that I could draw smiles and laughs from them pleasantly. So, everything was alright, and we set out to get the food items with Helen behind the wheel. Merely seconds after we got on the freeway, Helen said we should change plans and stop by an urgent care facility near the house. She reminded me that I had scheduled a follow-up visit with the resident doctor to review the results of the test they had done days before. Excited about the trip downtown, more so the dishes Helen would prepare, I suggested we go downtown first and then stop at the clinic on our way back.

However, Helen insisted we prioritize health, as downtown could wait. I sensed what she was saying and gave her my unspoken approval. We exited the freeway and headed to the clinic. She dropped me off at the entrance and went to find parking while I went to check in. Suddenly, I started feeling chills and physical unsteadiness at the check-in desk and thought everything would go away momentarily. Not so! By the time I was in the doctor's room, the chill level had worsened. My mouth began to quiver, and my hands and legs were shaking. The doctor came in and noticed something was wrong. "Are you okay?" he asked, concerned. This sudden turn of events was a shock to all of us.

I told him I was feeling cold, and he quickly informed his crew to increase the temperature in the room. This did not help, as I became more uncomfortable crossing and uncrossing my legs, hoping this would help. As the doctor was asking me questions about what and how I was feeling, I could not respond lucidly. I slurred with choppy and incomprehensible simple sentences. He quickly dashed out of the room to get Helen. They both rushed in, and the doctor checked my vitals —heart rate, pulse, and blood pressure. I was becoming less aware of my environment at this time, perhaps losing my consciousness. Seeing that I was shivering convulsively, Helen took off her jacket to cover me and then tightly held her chest to mine to ward off the shivering. She was nervous and scared, as I could feel her heart pounding. With a shaken voice, she repeatedly said to me that all would be well. According to the doctor, my heart rate was wildly high at 189. My eyes, skin, and palms turned visibly yellow. Worried and panicked, the doctor called the paramedics to assess the situation and possibly take me to the emergency room of a nearby hospital. Fifteen minutes later, while Helen was still shielding me, four paramedics rushed in and were briefed about the triggers. They soon began to take my vitals for their records. Somehow, the chills started to wane as soon as the paramedics entered. The shaking lessened, and I began to feel the warmth emanating from Helen's chest. The yellowness, however, remained. The urgency of the paramedics' actions was palpable, and it was clear that this was a serious situation.

After discussing the situation with the doctor, the paramedics decided to take me to an emergency room nearby for further examination and treatment. They placed me on the gurney and moved me into an ambulance. We rolled while they were taking more vitals and monitoring my general condition. They asked me questions to assess my alertness, and I answered, I believe, satisfactorily. Considering what happened, I was grateful to be able to function better in the ambulance. Not once did the paramedics fail me in their service. Everything was urgent and demanded their utmost attention. Intermittently, they asked how I was feeling, and I responded, "better." They all sympathetically said to me at intervals that all would be well. Their concern and consummate humanity touched me, and with tears streaming down my cheeks, I addressed all of them thus:

"Thank you. I appreciate what you have done for me. Care demands the best and the most we can give, and you have done that. Not everybody can do that; it takes a special person. You are special! May God bless you. Thank you."

Their eyes were focused on me, indicating their reciprocal appreciation of my sentiments. With his eyes welling up, one of the paramedics placed his hand on me and said, "We are almost there.

"You'll be fine." "Thank you," I said, choking up with emotion. The paramedics' comforting words and actions provided a much-needed sense of relief and reassurance amid the crisis.

At the hospital, the crew stayed with me and continued monitoring my vitals while waiting. Their boss showed up at the hospital—they must have called him—and was equally vested in my predicament. Once briefed by the crew, he approached me and asked how I was doing. He facilitated my prompt intake by the emergency room personnel. The usual paperwork and handing over were concluded, and the paramedics left, but not before they said goodbye to me. Undoubtedly, this was another pivotal moment for me, not only a moment but also a lifetime of appreciation for human empathy and shared humanity. By how the paramedics responded, I could tell they were good people worthy of emulation in their dedication to their calling.

Once I was released to the emergency room staff, they recognized the urgency in my case, appropriately so, and began working on me. There were tests upon tests, all kinds, including a series of blood tests at short intervals. There was a blood draw every 30 minutes.

My temperature, blood sugar, and urine were also assessed frequently. My emergency room space was open to all the staff. I saw different people come in at various times, with some coming more frequently than others. Each time I thought I could get a respite, the nurses came in to take my vitals, doctors checked my charts, in addition to offering updates, and cleaners were on hand to empty the trash cans and bio-hazard bins in the room. It was like clockwork, a constant cycle of actions.

Within four hours, the emergency crew drew my blood six times from both arms and hands. The urgency of the situation was evident. I remember jokingly saying to one of the nurses that I was being "Draculaized." She laughed and said they were doing that for a good reason; they had to determine what sent me to the emergency room.

As part of their diligence, the emergency room doctor contacted my doctor, who performed the surgery. The surgeon himself came to the emergency room to see me. Afterwards, he consulted with the emergency room doctors on what should be done. From where I was positioned, I saw the surgeon speaking to the emergency room crew and using the computer to document his recommendations. The surgeon came back to my bedside to brief me about his orders. First, according to him, they would do a CT scan and reinstall the drain removed days before, but only as warranted by the CT scan. He also told me that the catheter would be reinstalled, as I was having difficulty with urination. While the surgeon was still talking to me, Helen walked in. A few weeks earlier, she had met with the surgeon a few times. She exchanged pleasantries with him and then showed him an email that she had received from the urgent care doctor. The email was about the result of the test that had been done earlier at the urgent care. An infection, the stubborn and most resistant kind, was the culprit. Coincidentally, the surgeon and the ER doctors had just concluded the same. The surgeon explained that it was a serious blood infection and that only one specific antibiotic could defeat it, corroborated by the urgent care doctor's email. Concerned, I asked, "What if it doesn't work? "Let's hope it works," said the surgeon with a smile. Now, a rare and virulent blood infection appeared when I was seeing a brightening light in my recovery. It was deflating, of course, but I quickly toppled despair and replaced it with resolve, courage, and optimism.

The in-and-out went on for five hours, and still, there was no conclusive finding of the cause of the attack or infection. I was curious and wanted to know the cause of the sudden attack. I asked an attending nurse who came to draw my blood what the problem was, and she responded that only the doctor could tell me that. At this point, I invoked my patience, rationalizing that the crew was only being diligent in establishing what the problem was and how to treat it. And so, the wait continued. My palms, eyes, and skin were still yellow, and urination, especially on demand, was difficult. I began to frantically guess what could have caused the attack. I thought about an infected or failing liver and other wild but probable causes. Through it all, Helen was with me and offered physical and psychological safety. One of the nurses had informed me earlier that they would move me from the emergency room to the main floor of the hospital when a room became available, indicating that I would not be discharged the same day. This was okay with me, as I considered myself lucky to be alive. Having been told that they would confine me to the hospital that day, I urged Helen to get some rest at home. She was up early and looked worn out, although she did not mention it.

Not long after Helen left, around 7 pm, a nurse came in with a visible smile. "Your room is ready upstairs, and we are moving you there," she said. That, for me, was a baby step forward in the grand scheme of things. I was happy. Twenty minutes later, I was in my unshared hospital room. Unlike my emergency room space, the room had a big window that streamed in natural light, which I liked. There was a small TV on the wall north of me. To my right were a small desk and two chairs. This, I mused, would be my space for as long as I needed to be hospitalized. I had better adapt. I was grateful even to have that small space, my smaller world in a larger one then.

At the time they moved me to the hospital room, I had not eaten or drunk anything. According to the nurses, this was because of the tests that had to be done. I feared being placed on a liquid diet again, having gone through this dreadfully two weeks before. I would have to endure, I told myself. I was in suspense on two levels: not knowing when I would get back on solid foods and not knowing when I would be discharged.

It is everyone's prayer not to be confined to a hospital room. Ever since I was little, it has certainly been mine. Although they are a place for healing, hospitals expose the fragility of life and often remind us of, or bring us closer to, our mortality. As much as they suit us, they come with their dreariness. I remember discharging myself from the hospital when I was ten years old. I had only been hospitalized for a day when I decided to check out of the hospital. Although it was a familiar environment because my mom was one of the lead nurses at the hospital, the context was melancholic and depressing. When I could not take it anymore, I put on my clothes and sneaked out of the hospital. Hours later, they found me at home. That feeling of drabness and depression got me worried about when I would be released—in one day, two, three, four, or five?

At 67, I can no longer check myself out of the hospital, as the act itself is reckless, stupid, and incompatible with rationality. I would have to persevere to get through each day at the hospital. I have always espoused that time presents in two opposite forms: it favors us when we need more of it to make something happen, but it turns against us when we want something accelerated. It can be our friend or enemy. In this case, it was my adversary, as I wished to spend the shortest time possible at the hospital. To tackle this unfriendly challenge of time, I thought of things I could do to pass the time. The TV was there, and I could indulge and binge-watch. I am a moderate news junkie, but watching the news at times can become boring with repetition. I could engage in scattered reflections on the past and delightful projections on the future. I also thought about being in the moment, bantering with all the hospital workers coming into my room, in a way to recognize their humanity, dignity, and dedication. I adopted all three. Around 10 pm, I persuaded Helen to go home and be with our daughter. She reluctantly left, and I realized that the hospital room could never substitute for home. It was unhomely again. I was alone.

When Helen left, I defaulted to my plan. I watched the news on TV, ruminated on the past and the future, and drifted off into the early morning hours. The morning glow began filtering into the room through the huge window. I felt lucky that I could benefit from the freshness of a new day. The cycle of activities continued as usual. The nurses showed up periodically to check my vitals and administer doctor-ordered medication. They were all very friendly and gracious, not in any way touch-and-go with me. They showed their warmth and dedication by asking questions and engaging in relevant conversations. I, in turn, acknowledged their generosity of warmth with heartfelt appreciation, thanking them and letting them know that their line of profession, care, is the most demanding and worthy of gratitude.

There were funny moments too to lessen the intensity and seriousness of my situation, lighter moments of endearment between the patient and the caregiver. One instance was when one of the nurses referred to Helen as my daughter. Talking to me, she said, "Your daughter here..." She was in mid-sentence when Helen said with a smile, "I'm his wife." Also smiling, the nurse said, "Oops! I am sorry," Helen animatedly responded, "she got you back," talking to me. Earlier in the day, also in one of those lighter moments, I had guessed the age of the same nurse wrong by about seven years, implying that she looked older than her actual age. "Do I look that old?" the nurse asked with a smile. She got me on the same thing, thinking that Helen was my daughter. We all laughed at ourselves and our terrible guessing skills, bringing much-needed

lightheartedness to the room.

The day went on in its time track, leaving us to fill it with action or

inaction. I would be active, I reminded myself, despite my

confinement. Not too long afterwards, a man in his white medical

robe with a stethoscope around his neck walked in. I knew

immediately that he was a doctor, but this would be the first time I

saw him. He soft-spoke and had a sheet of crumpled paper with

scattered scribbles in hand. He introduced himself as an infection

expert. Taking notes, he began with questions and then continued

with a thorough and comprehensible explanation of his findings and

recommendations for treatment beyond medication. Just like my

surgeon had mentioned, he remarked that the infection was the

serious kind that would invade my blood and eventually take me out

if left untreated. According to him, my infection was why everyone

who came into my room had to wear a bio-hazard gown, which was

carefully removed and disposed of before the nurses left the room.

He further remarked that he, in concert with the other doctors, had

ordered an intravenous treatment of antibiotics for fourteen days, starting later in the day. He continued that they would monitor my progress or lack thereof for two days at the hospital, only releasing me to complete the rest of the days at home if they determined that the treatment was working. He explained with clarity, and I had no questions for him.

Two hours or so later, the nurses showed up in their biohazard gowns and started installing the disinfecting drip. I was needled again in the arm to create pathways for the antibiotics to get into my body. As usual, the nurses were very pleasant throughout the process.

Another medical directive soon came in for the catheter to be installed again. I had never seen it done while awake before and feared it could be painful. Indeed, it was, as the tube was being inserted. But with the catheter installed, the challenge of urination was eliminated, bringing a sense of relief and comfort.

Helen was in the room with me when a nurse came to write the updates on the whiteboard. My eyes were transfixed on the board because I wanted to know the updates. Then my eyes roved to the diet with the word "assorted" in front of it. I quickly directed Helen's attention to it. I had been looking forward to getting back to everyday foods. At last, it happened. I was pleased because I had only been on water for about thirty hours. We eventually ordered hospital food and celebrated by talking about light stuff, like our daughter's latest antics or the funny TV shows we missed. Sometimes, we even poked fun at ourselves, finding humor in our situation. Helen stayed with me until I prompted her to get some rest at home. As usual, she demurred and only yielded to please me. I felt for her, as she didn't get much rest between home and the hospital.

The treatment went on as usual, with the crew coming in at intervals to refill the IV, check my vitals, and administer medication. With Helen gone, I was back in my solo world. I caught the news on TV and backtracked to my childhood and adolescence in moments of therapeutic reflection. I was able to embrace and appreciate my past, good or bad, constructively to inform my future. This was calming, as I fell asleep in good spirits, feeling a sense of peace and acceptance, and better grounded in reality.

In the quiet morning hours, I woke up and felt I should do something other than watch TV or indulge in reflections. I was restless. Dreariness was brewing again, and I felt compelled to block it. I looked around the room and thought of the space (my hospital room) as a special gift I could use for something meaningful or beneficial. In recent years, finding something to do as a diversion in the tightest spaces and under the most challenging circumstances has become my life strategy. This is a way to escape the anguish I might be going through. So, to create a diversion, I got up and sat behind a small desk with the help of a nurse. I realized that this space, my hospital room, could be my office. In this place, I could write or record my thoughts, turning a potentially negative situation into a space for creativity and certitude. I voiced this in video recordings, transcribed thus:

Monologue 1 – Direct Address to Helen

It's another day on this recovery journey, and it has been turbulent. I pray it's a brief one. I've realized that life, especially during recovery, requires deliberate planning. It's not about crafting a grand, long-term plan, but about setting short-term goals and proceeding measuredly, in steps, on the road to recovery. This planning is crucial, as it keeps us from falling into the abyss of "planlessness," which can lead to "nothingness." So, I got up around 3 am and started writing, and with that, my mind was taken off what was a threat to me then. I was lost in that writing. I was in another world. I was in my space and did not allow anything else to come in. After that, my thoughts became clearer, and I thought about you, and I mean you, Helen. You have displayed your love, and it's so clear and glaring. Your exceptionality is unquestionable to me because of what you have shown me, what you have expressed, and what you have done. I appreciate you for that in no small measure. The evidence is overwhelming. Thank you. I feel relieved having said this because it was like a tipping point regarding the streams of my consciousness and conscience. I am relieved that I have gotten it out. Let us hope for the best today, as always. Optimism now swells in my world, and, as it does, gulps up pessimism. I am not one for negativism anymore, although I know it is present; I don't have to indulge in it or allow it to thrive. I must move on confidently, not being naïve, not ignoring it, but placing hope and efforts, as well as determination, ahead of it. This is an effective way to rob it of its energy to make room for optimism. That's what I'm doing right now. This has been a rough ride, but we'll survive it. We'll triumph. Thank you, Helen.

You need to take care of yourself, too. I remember that the doctor told you to be careful, as your body could attract virulent bacteria in me. You didn't panic! You didn't fret. You remained there for me. Everyone who came into the room had the protective suit on except you. Even when I told you to wear the suit, you shrugged it off. Of what stock is your faith in the face of fear? I presume high grade, as you have emerged unscathed a few times you have done this. This is not your usual self; this side of you only shows up in the context of care for our daughter and me. It must be love overriding fear. Thank you. You are an exemplary person. You present with grace, empathy, love, and care. Whatever the challenge is, especially this one, we will ride it out with your vibes and vigor. We are almost there. The haze will clear, and you and I will loom larger to be real. Thank you.

Monologue 2 – A Direct Address to Myself

Welcome to my office! This is where I am right now (hospital room), and I can make the place anything I want. The therapist just left and certified me as steady and ready regarding my physical fitness. Progress! For the rest of the day, I will work in my office, my hospital room. It's perfect. You can see the gorgeousness of the day through the big window, creating inner peace. It's a misty morning, a bit somber, but in that somberness is calmness. This is home for now, and I just must adapt to it, making sure that it doesn't take all of me because I have a home that can nurture me better than this when my health is restored. It's always good to make the best use of any context, anywhere we find ourselves. I got up this morning and started writing, and throughout the day, I'll be writing, looking ahead, not looking back.

I have a lot of rumination to do, a lot of introspection, and a lot of appreciation to tender. God has always been good. I see every challenge in our lives as a test, a test of our faith, a test of our will, and a test of who we are. I thank God for this circumstance, this dilemma of illness, because it offers a big life lesson. Life is a blend of bitterness and sweetness, an amalgam of the odds and the good things, a mixture of normal and abnormal, and a hodgepodge of challenges and achievements. It's never one way with life. So, the mist this morning will clear, and it will yield to that cloudless day. May today be clear for everyone. Let's look beyond now to get to the other side, but we must deal with the now. This is me dealing with the now in this space, my hospital room.

Monologue 3 – A Direct Address to the Hospital Crew (Homage to Caregivers)

I will be remiss if I do not mention the top-notch care I have received here at the hospital. Everyone, from cleaners to doctors, has been tremendously caring, friendly, compassionate, and resolute. All of you have awakened my nascent humanity, and I know I'll be better for it. I was enveloped in your smiles, wrapped in your care, swaddled by your warmth, and secure in your compassion. I was free and plain with all of you because your humanity was that appreciable.

A nurse took care of me yesterday, and just like the rest of you, left me with a memorable impression of human decency and dignity in the purview of care and interactions with others. Tall, moderately tattooed, and well-built, she came in and was all business. Although she said good morning to me, her face did not show genuineness in what she said. I wondered if she was as pleasant as the rest of them. Based on her serious countenance, my mind started drifting, and I queried what kind of person she was and what could have been the reason for her being like that. All the while, she kept busy doing what she was doing. At one point, I saw her watching the news on the screen. It was political content, the kind that makes people take sides and judge others by their acquired biases.

There was silence between us, as our eyes were intensely trained on the screen. Peripherally, I looked at her face and saw it was still inscrutable. Could the news bit I was watching be out of the range of her affiliations? Could it also be that she was assessing me as I was observing her? The wondering kept on, increasingly simmering into my judgment of her. My mind went to the extreme: she must not like my kind, I thought. I felt a sag in my heart that I had to be this extreme. It was not the right way to think or believe without glaring evidence. After a few minutes of wondering between us, I saw a glimmer of ease. She turned to me and remarked, "You are doing much better, my friend. The infection is responding to the antibiotics."

Looking away from the computer screen, she continued, "It won't be long now; you will be cleared of the infection if your progress continues." I pray so," I said. "It will be if you believe," she said confidently. We went into other things, my profession, prevailing events, and personal philosophy about care and humanity. "It takes a special person to do what you do. I could tell you are at peace with yourself doing what you do," I shared with her. "Well, what joy is there if you don't love what you are doing? It's the blood that flows in life and the engine that makes life go. I have been doing this for years and still enjoy being here every day, seeing and appreciating the essence of life. It's somehow rewarding to care," she said. "It is so in education as well, in every profession requiring human interactions," I responded. She asked if I needed anything else. I said no and thanked her for sparing the time and emotions to engage. Her aura was so powerful and sincere that I forgot about my health conundrum. Psychologically, she was like an unprescribed medication that relieved me of my agonies. She was more than I thought of her; she stood out among her peers and was, and still is, a reminder of how we should all be around people.

Another reminder or lesson from my interaction with her is not to judge people before you get to know them. I misread her and allowed my unfiltered sense of stereotypes to put me in overdrive, assuming rather than waiting for evidence and judging without proof. Although I have consciously avoided this behavior, it occasionally finds me. It's unintellectual and shows one's lack of discipline to tame this behavior. Additionally, I see this insensitivity as limiting learning and growth. When you think you know and know nothing, all you know is nothing. I wouldn't have benefited from the largess of her humanity had I held on to my bias and had she not related to me. The ones who proffer benevolence and relate freely with the rest of us, like the nurse did, elevate our humanity.

An hour later, the nurse showed up again to let me know that her shift was over and she was leaving. She asked if I wanted her to do or get anything for me. I told her that her patience, compassion, care, and humanity would last me a lifetime. She was an example of who to be, what to be, and how to be. She exited the room, but what she left behind is now lodged firmly in me.

The Nurse: Icon of Humanity

The lasting influence of my nurse friend, a person I may never cross paths with again, was a catalyst that guided my interactions with the hospital staff who came in after her. Her presence instilled in me a greater sense of openness and a willingness to embrace people's inherent goodness, while encouraging me to present the best version of myself. This experience taught me that such interactions never leave us at a deficit; they only serve to enrich our lives.

Helen returned later in the day and surprised me with the food I had been craving, knowing that I had just been liberated from the sorry liquid diet I had been on. Delightfully, we settled down and indulged, reminiscing, laughing at ourselves, and talking about our shared future. I spoke about my nurse friend, stressing the inspiration she aroused in me and regretting how I allowed my unfiltered bias to infer negative things about her erroneously. She commented that there was nothing to regret, as the experience allowed me to learn, a chance for my flaws and imperfections to be revealed for corrections. I perceived the sense in what she said and was thankful that my bias was exposed in a way for me to work against it. As ordinary or basic as it is, deconstructing or evaluating our biases is necessary for learning and growth.

At some point, with the benefit of the good experiences I had at the hospital, I began to increasingly see my hospital room, my space, as a good ground to heal, change, and grow. Then the news came that I might be discharged the next day because my infection was responding well to the antibiotics. This news delightfully flavored the good feeling I had been having, a new outlook.

As the day wore on, Helen and I manifested our good vibes by discussing various things, which felt good. Shared challenges can indeed generate benign mutuality in our shared space. It was just the two of us against cancer, with God unfailingly presiding over our fate. We were elated and thankful that I could be released the next day. Daylight began to fade, and the dusk claimed its place in the framework of time. Through the huge glass window in my room, I saw a beautiful, amber sky forming, more attractive than the experts' paintings. For moments, it took over my mind peacefully and spiritually—metaphorically, maybe, my gradual liberation from cancer. It also tracked time and brought me closer to my impending release the next day.

Feeling lucky and good, Helen and I ordered dinner from the hospital kitchen, not necessarily because we were hungry, but to distinguish the moment by showing solidarity in the face of adversity. We ate and left nothing uneaten. It was the good feeling more than hunger that made us eat.

The next day, I woke up to the morning's glory, with the beautifully refracted sun's rays filtering into the room, another opportunity for me to appreciate the magnificence of nature. Even with its wrath, nature has always been a phenomenon of wonder and tremendous appeal to me. At its best, it grants me calm, balance, inspiration for creativity, patterns, grandeur, and more. In its impact this morning, the sun granted me all, imbuing me with enormous gratitude. I considered my discharge later in the day a new door that opened to a more fulfilling life. Soon, it was time for me to be discharged. The nurses came and apprised me of the dos and don'ts of discharge.

Helen was my backup ears and mind as usual, assuring that whatever I couldn't get, she would. Before leaving the hospital, we prayed aloud that the experience wouldn't repeat itself and that it wouldn't be the revolving type. It was harrowing!

Home was what I thought it would be—a familiar, cozy, comforting, and private place, especially with my daughter and Helen. Picking up from where we left off, we continued our routine daily activities- breakfast, lunch, dinner, Helen helping with bathing, intermittent outings, discussing, watching interesting programs, etc. There was one special thing we had to do that was new, though. As part of our briefing at the hospital, the nurses told us that the intravenous antibiotics had to be continued at home. I had to be on the medication for fourteen days altogether, out of which I spent two days at the hospital.

For monitoring and care purposes, home health nurses were contracted for two days weekly, with Helen filling in as a surrogate for twelve days. Helen had to learn the administration process quickly, as the instructing nurse only showed up once. During instruction, I remember thinking that the process was intimidating with several apparatuses and steps involved. Besides, everything required accuracy, diligence, and meticulousness. Frankly, I doubted whether one instruction session would be enough for anyone to master. Thinking that the reason for the process was a severe infection demanding the utmost urgency, I was nervous. Helen, however, assured me that she would have no difficulty administering the medication as instructed. On her first day of administration, she carefully sequenced the gadgetry according to the steps in the guide. She then began the administration process as instructed, ascertaining that she followed each step accordingly.

By the third day, I observed that we were spending less time doing what we had to do. Forty-five minutes soon became thirty minutes. Helen had gained fluency and efficiency, which could be ascribed to practice. I wasn't surprised because some of her positive attributes were manifested in her handling of the process. She is determined, observant, and learns fast. I was radiantly pleased with her.

For about three weeks, my recovery was normal without any incidents warranting hospital visits. At different moments each day, I was supplicantly asking God to bar any situation that would send me back to the hospital. Helen and I were also careful, following instructions carefully, eating appropriately, medicating on time, and doing everything else that could maintain my recovery trend. Then I began to feel pain in the area where they had inserted the catheter. It started mildly and then became unbearable. At the slightest movement, I flinched and cringed.

As the pain intensified, burning became more pronounced and unendurable. I couldn't sleep at night, and ordinary daily activities presented difficulty. I couldn't sit without grimacing, I couldn't stand up without feeling the pain, and I couldn't get in and out of the car without feeling a sting. I was miserable, as I was robbed of many moments of comfort or ease. The pain was not just physical; it was a constant, unwanted companion, affecting my mood, my ability to concentrate, and my relationships. At first, I localized the treatment by resorting to pain relievers, burn ointment, Icy Hot, and other pain-reducing agents, but nothing worked. The agonies would soon move from a bother to that of a red-alert concern. It was urgent that we move from a localized, self-managed treatment to a medically supervised alternative. I could tell that the catheter was the cause of my pain, but the treatment was the major challenge. I shared with Helen that I was tired of the catheter because I had been wearing it for too long and that it was causing me more problems as opposed to relief. At times, I mouthed out loud painfully that the catheter had to be disconnected for me to be better. Rather than see it as a friend, I saw it as a foe. It was clear I had to submit to the experts.

On the morning of my birthday, May 23, Helen and I decided it would be best to check into an ER again, which I had dreaded all along. The day before, we had planned to have a low-brow birthday at a neighborhood restaurant, a place of familiarity more appealing to our prevailing emotions than other restaurants. It was the most suitable for our mood at the time. We had both looked forward to dining at the restaurant. Better at prioritizing than I am in most cases, Helen suggested we go to the ER and skip dining at the restaurant. It was instantly sensible for us to do this. We did and headed to the ER. We checked in and were given an estimated wait time of one and a half to two hours. We were hungry and hadn't eaten anything in deference to eating at the restaurant. We figured we had enough time to dine at the restaurant while waiting for our slot at the ER. So, to the restaurant we went. We had our meal and experienced the attendant calming vibes associated with our experience there. We returned to the ER and did not lose our place in the queue. We were able to combine both objectives with time as our benefactor. We felt good.

In the ER, the doctors there asked me questions about my pain dilemma, and I, with my explanation, implicated the catheter, not as an excuse to get rid of it but as the most obvious cause. I could tell where the pain was coming from because pain itself is easily traceable. One can always tell where it hurts. In addition to asking me questions, the doctors evaluated my medical records, including available ER history. They extended their efforts by consulting with my surgeon, who, in concert with them, decided that the catheter be removed. When the doctors told me about their decision, I felt relieved that the source of my pain would be eliminated. The relief was not just physical; it was mental and emotional. Within minutes, they took out the catheter, and I felt mentally energized again. An unnatural, foreign agent that had its usefulness but could be inconvenient and risky (infection) was removed.

Free of the catheter and with the pain gradually reducing, I went back home with Helen to enjoy the gift of this birthday, relief!

Though low-brow and somber, the significance of this birthday

outstripped that of the previous ones I had had, with its grand gift of

relief. There's nothing as significant as relief from ill health. With the

pain eliminated, my daily activities assumed normalcy, and I started

planning to return to work. I had been off for almost three months as

ordered by my surgeon. I made a couple of visits to the surgeon's

office following some tests. Upon reviewing the test results, the

surgeon certified me ready for work. The clearance to return to work

was a significant milestone in my recovery, lifting my spirits. Even

though I had been busy at home doing things requiring my intellect,

not physical strength, I still felt underproductive. I missed the

workplace interactions, the procedural demands, and the opportunity

and vibrancy of learning daily amid others.

Returning to Work

Returning to work marked another stride in my recovery. It was a more measurable way of assessing it. I returned to work in the first week of June, about three months after my pre-surgery process. I was happy. I could have stayed a few more days at home to close the school year, but I thought that would have been a downer. I wanted something upbeat that would signify hope and freshness, not staleness, which would reconnect me with the people who have always been the bedrock of my growth, my students. When I told them that I was going to have surgery, they showed me unfettered empathy. Some wrote letters—I have taught college and university classes for thirty-six years—and handed them to me in class. I was touched by their sentiments and glad that they were able to find a purpose for the writing skills they had acquired. Other students privately registered their empathetic sense verbally, with some wishing me well with prayers. They all showed me that we were connected by bigger things than the curriculum, pedagogy, main idea, and details; we were connected by our humanity.

Returning to Work

I made a good decision to close the academic year with these wonderful people. They received me well with grace, a sense of shared triumph, and blissful co-existence. It would have been a letdown had I not returned to work to close out the year with them. It was my way of acknowledging and appreciating a significant touch of humanity. I can say doubtlessly that this, in a sense, advanced my recovery and outlook in general.

My recovery continued in the right direction, and I started planning my usual summer trips, fervently praying that no health crisis would be a blockade. All the follow-up screenings I had done were favorable, strengthening my determination to travel. I told Helen and my daughter to go to Africa before me, and that I would join them two weeks later. The anticipation of these trips filled me with excitement and hope for the future.

A day before Helen and my daughter's departure, I felt the onset of pain in my pelvic area. Again, I dismissed it as temporary and hoped it would go away later in the day. Pain like this had happened before and then would disappear. This pain, however, lingered and worsened, affecting my ambulation. It slowed my movement and made my gait and walking awkward. A walk that would normally take me three minutes would triple the time. The pain didn't relent and only became more of a handicap for me. Things as simple or basic as putting on my clothes became more demanding and excruciatingly painful. I was worried that the cycle of discomfort would come back again. What now? It felt and looked like a pattern, a dreaded replay of hope that devolved into hopelessness. "When would I get a break?" I asked silently many times. I took my concern to my urgent care doctor, and he prescribed a muscle-relaxing pill, in addition to urging me to stay on Tylenol consistently. More importantly, he advised me to get a soft, padded seat cushion to help relieve the pressure on my tailbone, as that may have triggered the pain. That made sense, as I had not been cushioning my seat. I made a scheduled visit to my surgeon two days later, and he also attributed my pain to the pressure on my tailbone. According to him, my surgery happened in my tailbone area, which could make sitting more problematic, often resulting in pain.

My surgeon reassured me that this type of post-surgery discomfort was not uncommon. He advised patience and caution and, most importantly, informed me that full recovery could take three to six months. This timeline, coming from the expert himself, brought relief. I was still within the expected recovery period for the type of surgery I had undergone.

My work requires a long sitting time daily, and, by this time, I had been back to work for three weeks on a special assignment. I would sit for up to five hours daily in an uncushioned chair, impacting my surgical area. Therefore, the explanation that the urgent care doctor gave was not far-fetched at all. So, I went looking for a medically recommended cushion. I bought two, one for the car and the other for the house. The cushions helped to reduce the pain slightly, but not fast enough. I was still concerned as I was painstakingly going through my daily activities. I didn't skip any activities, such as work responsibilities or chores at home. I swept and mopped the floor daily, made the bed every morning, and prepared my meals twice or thrice daily. I did everything with determination and a never-quit attitude. I didn't see the pain as an excuse for not performing. I may have accomplished more with the pain than when I didn't have it. Occasionally, though, I felt dispirited about the slow pace of recovery, wondering if I could travel as planned. Thirty-four hours total flight time (round trip) with two connections, multiple immigration, customs, and TSA checks seemed too much for the little energy I had. There was also the risk of developing something else or worsening the existing problem.

All these worries got me to reevaluate my planned trip. I began to think it through on my own, imagining all the things that could go wrong while traveling. The imagery was scary, and I became increasingly apprehensive about leaving my little comfort behind. A week before I would travel, it became improbable that I would take the plunge, especially with the concerns of friends and family members, including Helen's. I finally got there; I decided to sit out the summer months at home in the States. This was a difficult decision for me to arrive at because I had promised my wife and daughter that I would be with them in Africa. To renege on this promise was harrowing for me. With their understanding, however, I forgave myself, cognizant of how health could precede or supersede the best of our plans and intentions.

Returning to Work

I began to accept this change in plans, increasingly dedicating

myself to my work assignments, chores, and personal pursuits at

home. For example, I had four books going at once, including this

one, and would bounce from one to another depending on my

creative flow and ideas at different times. Creating, imagining, and

elevating my aura above my dilemma was pleasing. I was

psychologically safe in my private world, which offered an outlet for

my passion. This private world fortifies our outer world of

interactions with others. I could feel this working in my daily life, as

I became more of what I had always wanted to be, a simply decent

human being who would see himself in others and others in himself.

Life became palpably more blissful.

At this point, I'm still recovering; there has been no traumatic

episode for three weeks now, and I pray nothing like that shows up.

In parallel with recovery, I'm doing everything I enjoy doing,

interacting with people appreciably without harboring rancor,

nurturing faith and spirituality, pursuing my interests, sponsoring and

sustaining determination, seeing opportunity in all situations,

meeting the hardest of times with constructive efforts, accepting the problem but not the defeat, and never wallowing in self-pity, saying "Why me?" I'm now in that corrective mode where "Why not me?" serves my interest more than "Why me?" It allows me to claim ownership of my problem by imposing responsibility to do something about it. Based on my evaluation, this life model, "Why not me?" has been inwardly and outwardly rewarding for me.

Challenges of Others: You Are Not Alone

It's one of my postulates these days that life is incomplete, or even "unlife-like," without challenges. Although we all hate problems in our lives, they are the most virile agents of change if we are committed to solving them or doing something constructive about them. I have experienced this multiple times in my life, including in my current fight against cancer. I have also witnessed this in the struggles of friends and family members against illnesses of various kinds.

I have a friend who, years ago, was diagnosed with a severe heart malfunction. It started slowly with water in his lungs, then spiraled to worse things. Following a moderate surgery to fix his lungs, he got better briefly and slipped back into the same heart challenge. There was swelling of his feet, along with unrelenting fatigue, notoriously symptomatic of a failing heart. He went for numerous tests and never once missed his medical appointments. He did everything the doctors instructed him to do, including daily walks. According to him, his doctors made him understand the severity of his condition and how important it was for him to help himself while they were helping him. He would tell me years later that he had to

adhere to everything the doctors wanted him to do, mainly because

he wished to live. I had never seen him take things as seriously as

this. While I was not surprised, I was impressed with his dedication

to and determination about what he needed to do for himself. Where

others would cheat, he would do more than he was asked. Despite all

he did, his condition did not show much improvement, but he fought

on. His doctors gave him an assortment of options, among which

was open heart surgery, the most extreme of the possibilities in terms

of risks. While surgery could fix the problem, according to the

doctors, it was the most invasive and risky of all the options.

Furthermore, the doctors informed him that the rest of the options

would not fix the problem but could buy him a few more years, up to

five. Determined to get more than five years and correct the

condition once and for all, he chose surgery, the high-risk option.

The doctors soon started the pre-surgery process involving serial

tests and screenings. During this preparatory process, he gave me

complete details about what he would go through. For instance, a

machine would be his breathing surrogate during surgery. He would not be able to breathe by himself, just like being dead. This was scary when he told me, as it could be for anyone.

On the eve of the surgery, around midnight, my phone rang. It was an unusual call, as people rarely called at that time. The call was from him. I knew instantly that there must have been a reason for the call. I answered it and asked if he was okay. He responded affirmatively, but his voice and tone gave him away. He sounded dour and somber. "What are you doing up at this time?" I asked again. He said he couldn't sleep and was drinking beer. "Beer?" I queried. According to him, he was afraid that he might not make it through surgery, as something could go wrong. So, he thought of drinking beer for the last time. He was afraid. I had never known him to be fearful of anything in the entire three decades of our friendship. In his defeated, weary, and worried voice, he continued that the reason for the call was that he had given my name to his doctors to call me in case the surgery didn't go well and they needed someone to authorize them to pull the plug. "Please, do it!" I don't want to be on life support or be a burden to anyone. I'd rather go. Please, do it! I'm sorry," he said in a deflated voice. Pulverized by his fear and the awkwardness of the moment, I had nothing to say

other than to assure him that he would make it with God on his side.

For the first time in our friendship, he didn't cast any doubt on what

God could do. It was difficult to end the call, but I had to leave him

in the hands of God. I couldn't sleep that night, troubled by the

specter of death. Death became more present and realistic as I saw

him wandering in my circle.

I must have called his wife ten times on the day of the surgery,

wanting to know how things were going. My fear became crazily

heightened when he was in surgery, more so when it went into

overtime. When I called, his wife told me she was still waiting. I

tensed up and was a wreck emotionally. Would I have to give that

dreadful go-ahead to the doctors? I prayed not.

Each time my phone rang, I panicked with a pounding heart.

Luckily, none of the calls were from the wife yet. I summoned the

courage to call again three hours past the estimated surgery duration.

The wife gladly told me they had moved him from the surgical room

to a recovery room. I was relieved with a feeling of triumph. It was a new day, even though it was late afternoon. It was a new beginning, far removed from the bleakness of the day before.

I went to see him at the hospital the next day. He was alert and could mutter a few words. One could tell that he had been through a lot. I could also see that he was delighted to be back. He was weak, but he wanted to talk. With the approval of the nurse in attendance, he showed me the work that the surgeon had done. It was too much to look at, as a large area of his chest and abdomen was heavily bandaged. Although terrified, I was humbled and better grounded by the sight of his surgical cuts.

That was my friend in that gruesome condition. He didn't ask for it but was saddled with it. He faced it bravely and emerged on the better side of his struggles. If it could happen to him, it could happen to me, too, as I was no better than he was in any way. In a sense, knowing about his struggles reinforced my resolve to confront hardship with valor instead of despondency.

While I was still with him in the recovery room, his surgeon sauntered in, sipping his coffee, all smiles and confidence. It was evident that he was not worried about anything. He briefly conversed with my friend about his recovery, exuding confidence by letting

him know that the worst was over. I was well immersed in the

moment as I had never witnessed that level of confidence in anyone,

let alone in a surgeon who had just done one of the most invasive

and frightening medical procedures. I remembered that my friend

had told me things about him before, especially his expertise,

geniality, and confidence in his skills. For example, he told me that

the surgeon, as an indication of his sureness, once assured him that if

anything went wrong, it would not be due to his skills but a machine

malfunction, which, according to him, was highly unlikely. My

friend further informed me that the surgeon only said this after he

had explained the procedure to him, letting him know the risks

involved and his chances of survival. Hearing about the scariness of

the procedure and the gloomy survivability rate was distressing for

him, but the exuded confidence of the surgeon filled him with hope

and stamina. There was nothing the surgeon hid from my friend. He,

the surgeon, encouraged him to seek second and even third opinions

from other specialists. This, of course, generated increased assurance

for my friend. So, when I met the surgeon in the recovery room, I instantly became an admirer based on my friend's accounts of him. I sidled up to him in the room and thanked him for his expertise in his craft and exemplary human relations attributes, his exceptional care, from which we can all learn. In the vast scheme of things, this is another example of what and how to be in any profession and our interactions with others.

For me today, my friend is an example of who to be, what to be, and how to be in the throes of life's hardships. His journey of struggles was, and remains, a resourceful and instructive tool or template in my own tussle with health and in life in general.

I have realized that many of my friends and family members, especially those in my age bracket, are going through all kinds of health issues in their lives. This affirmation of life's uncertainty has made me appreciate life more. There was a time we didn't think or talk about death as frequently as we do now. We were younger, healthier, and well-steeped in life, not anymore in the wake of age and associated illnesses. I think I'm better for it, though, as I'm now grounded in the basics of life, not the pomp, which translates into peace and bliss. I am now "wisened," not wizened, by challenges and the will to overcome them.

I have another friend, a dear friend, who is now going through his health scare bravely with demonstrable faith. If a health crisis could befall anyone, it would not, and should not, be this friend. His character is clean and consistent, and his faith is unwavering. Retired, he is actively involved in church affairs and has earned knighthood in the Catholic context. He's a family man committed to his children and grandchildren. His family sense also extends to his friends. For over thirty years, I have been a perennial beneficiary of his friendship, compassion, propriety, empathy, and generosity. I met him on an equal level through his wife, also a cherished friend. The friendship has blossomed over the years from friendship to familyhood, with their children doubling as mine and mine as theirs. We talk about life, growth, and spirituality in the context of family and life. We are consistently enamored in the company of one another. I call him "my master" for many reasons, particularly his consistency in faith. However, he does not overwhelm others with his faith. He is highly sociable and loves to entertain and bring people together. At gatherings, he is the one who offers everything to everyone tirelessly, showing a high sense of savoir-faire. He is a rare model, even as he is facing his health dilemma now. His resilience in the face of this crisis is truly inspiring.

According to his wife, the crisis unexpectedly showed up. There was no warning, no suspicion, and there were no symptoms. It dawned suddenly. They had made plans to do certain things, among which were travel and faith work. It was through a routine health check that they found out. It was puzzling and heart-rending, and they had to go through a series of checks to confirm the adversarial health condition initially suspected. They paused on everything and made this crisis their central action. Travels were out, along with many other things. Suddenly, their world turned 180 degrees, meaning they had to abandon everything and adopt new and uncomfortable things. It was difficult for everyone in the family, more so for my ailing friend, who had to adapt to a frightful and grueling situation.

Like in my case, they initially kept their challenge to themselves out of respect for people's emotions, time, and daily challenges. I learned about their situation when they called to check on me. They had been calling before then but didn't tell me what they were going through. They had even asked to come and see me, but my isolation (due to infection) was restrictive. As we talked, my friend's wife disclosed what they were dealing with. The diagnosis was cancer of a rare kind, invading the blood and capable of taking down the organs aggressively. She outlined the treatment steps for me, which would require them to be housed in isolation at a cancer treatment center for weeks, even months. I asked how my friend was doing, and his wife informed me that things had been worrisome and episodic, but he was hopeful, powered by his faith. Every day was a challenge, but he had more courage and faith than the challenges could endure. I asked to speak with him, but I couldn't because his condition was so severe that he couldn't get on the phone.

I was devastated and wondered why my friends and I were experiencing health challenges at the same time. I began to see his struggles as mine and mine as his. In my prayers, it was no longer I but we. I felt the vigor of his faith and the courage in his determination. More than ever, I was determined to transcend my challenge, partly driven by our will, his and mine.

My friend is faring better, following intensive treatment requiring draining and replacing blood and other things in his body. According to his wife, the doctors did this for weeks while administering chemotherapy. It was a delicate undertaking that demanded caution and even restraint. No one was allowed around him except his wife, for care, and the necessary hospital personnel. Even his children and grandchildren were barred. They still can't be in proximity, and his outings are limited to a daily walk in the immediate neighborhood with his wife, while heavily masked. I have seen them twice since I learned about their ordeal, but from a distance. They were on the porch while I was standing in the street by my car. We were happy to see one another after a long time, though we were reduced to waving instead of hugging. We shared the moment touchingly, bonded by our friendship, struggles, and humanity. The candid vibe of acceptance, courage, gratitude, and faith despite adversity was clear in the two visits. "It has been rough, wearing, and dire, but God is our strength, our rock," shared the wife.

My friend is still going through his recovery, as I am. We talk every so often, mostly about how lucky we are to be here, to be afforded the opportunity to be the best of ourselves in any situation. The things that used to be in focus for us are now out of focus, leaving us with the essentials, the simple things that constitute life's fulcrum and make for bliss. Why would it take our challenges to come to this realization? We sometimes wonder, often circling back to the reality that hardships, in and of themselves, are not anathema to life but necessary to burnish it based on one's response to it. Our talks are like a spiritual session grounded in faith, dressed in candor, and driven by our relevant individual experiences and those of others. It's been healing and life changing. Our recovery continues, not necessarily limited to recovery from our health battles, but also from ourselves, playing up the simple things in life while downplaying the glare and flare, the pomp.

The Kaiser Man: Faith and Hope Personified

Learning occurs around us daily unless we choose to ignore it. Many of us ignore it most of the time by being unmindful of the context. Many instances in our lives are free and resourceful, often enriching our lives. Such situations have happened several times in my life, most of which I have ignored. I have also experienced a few that I can describe as good examples of what I ought to be or do. One such thing happened recently when I accompanied a sick friend to the hospital.

The hospital lobby was bustling on this day. Some people looked fit and healthy, and others were visibly ailing. Except for the workers, everybody was there for health reasons. I looked around, constantly observing everyone and wondering what specific challenges each person had. How did they feel about their illness? How were they dealing with it in the context of daily demands? Was their illness terminal? These and many other questions crossed my mind. I saw people saying hello and conversing without knowing one another. I also observed that people gladly left their seats for the feebler ones among us. The smiles were broad and genuine, fostering mutual respect and hope. It was pleasant to watch. I wondered what prompted this benign behavior. Was it the vulnerability that people felt about their health battles? Could the people there see themselves in one another because of their dilemma?

As I sat in the guest area, my friend was directed to occupy one of the spaces. I noticed that all the technicians there were friendly. They greeted us with smiles, fist-bumps, and some delightful banter. I felt a surge in my spirits and was overtaken by good feelings. However, that was not all. Two minutes later, a medium-built man, walking with a cane in his right hand, perhaps in his early or late fifties, came in and began talking, his voice filling the room. From the moment he walked in and opened his mouth, all eyes were on him. At first, I was skeptical. What could this man possibly have to say that would impress me? But as he spoke, I was drawn in by his infectious optimism. His words, combined with the welcoming and supportive environment of the hospital, created a space filled with positive vibes and human connection.

"How's everyone in here doing today? Thank God it's a beautiful day. The sun is shining, and it's bright out there. Can you feel it? It's

God's gift to us all; we must make it work for others. Life is good, no matter what," he said. He connected with everyone in the room, making eye contact, fist-bumping, and smiling. His upbeat attitude was transmissible. I had just been writing on my phone about optimism and good-naturedness when this man walked in. I connected with him immediately, as did everyone else in the room. He was the living example of the power of faith and hope. Everything that came from his mouth was uplifting and delivered with human genuineness. Like everybody else, he was there because of his health issue, but he didn't let his challenges rob him of the best he had to offer.

As he left the room, I stood up to shake his hand, thanking him for brightening not just my day, but perhaps my entire outlook on life with his infectious buoyancy. His demeanor had a tangible impact, as the room was filled with genial conversations. A patient sitting next to me whispered that the man had cancer, a type that would often make a comeback, but his optimism was always touching. The patient further stated that he had seen the man many times before at the hospital, and he was the same embodiment of optimism each time. This experience made me reflect on the power of humanity and the resilience of the human spirit. It reminded me that no matter the challenges we face, we always have the choice to approach life with optimism and kindness. For me, what the man demonstrated was nothing short of spirituality.

Spirituality and Faith

The word spirituality now appears more frequently in my conversations and discourse with people, and I know why: it reveals and drives my state of mind. The mind, I believe, doesn't stray from what it shows or says. In the realm of spirituality, I'm evolving. So, what does spirituality mean to me? In the context of my experiences and those of others in a reflective mode, I posit that spirituality is not a religion, although it offers a pathway to it. It is earthbound primarily and entrenched in our interactions with others and nature. In a sense, it is our beliefs and practices, individually and collectively. It is characterized by harmlessness, fairness, and propriety. It is a persistent and consistent sense of goodness. It is discipline and liberation of the mind. When you are spiritual, you are free from all the baggage around you. It empowers you to be wholesome and lets you see things clearly and beautifully, with purity and harmlessness toward others. We can find it in people, nature, and everything around us. When it dawns, it bestows bliss and heralds satisfaction and confidence. It is the undercurrent of one's good character that strengthens faith. It is a tenet, a way of life for us to be in harmony with ourselves, others, and nature.

Spirituality begins with the individual, with self-awareness as its cornerstone. It's the understanding that being good to oneself, not selfishly, naturally extends to others. Conversely, if one struggles within, navigating the larger world becomes a challenge, let alone making a positive impact.

In its greater force, spirituality is a precursor or an element of religious faith. It can strengthen one's religion in terms of faith and how it's demonstrated. You can't have one without the other and expect to be a model for your religion, any religion. For example, "Love thy neighbor as you love yourself" is spiritual in that it's about life, our world, and is extendable to our religious faith and practices. I believe you can't be a wholesome Christian or Muslim if you are a misanthrope, a person who hates humankind. Spirituality, however, doesn't have to be connected to any religious faith; it can stand alone or be found in people who don't espouse any religion and those who hold traditional beliefs.

A friend of mine recently shared a story that illustrates this. He and I have been fascinated with observing people around us in multiple situations for years. These observations have been very instructive in our lives, especially in how we see life and our interactions with others, believing that it takes the people around us—what we see and what they do—and nature for us to learn, change, and grow.

The story goes that my friend, in the company of two younger relatives, went to one of the remaining elders of his family to inform him about the funeral arrangements for his stepmother. According to my friend, he hadn't seen this 90-year-old uncle in years and had no idea how he would be received. My friend introduced himself and was asked by the uncle whose son he was among the relatives. This is lineage tracing, which is especially important in the African context. It is not enough to know that you are related to someone; it is also essential to understand how you are related. My friend shared some details about his dad with the uncle, who then recalled with appreciation all the good things my friend's dad had done for him when he was younger, praising my friend's dad's altruism and praying for the same to be replicated in his progeny. In a spiritual—

some will say—traditional way, the uncle directed his grandson to bring out a bottle of schnapps. This liquor is commonly used to offer prayers and welcome guests in the spirit of goodness and humanity. It is also symbolic of transparency, humility, and sincerity in reverence for fellow humans and nature.

Following his prayer, a long, poetic, rhythmic monologue replete with allegorical and metaphoric references about humans and nature, the uncle offered them drinks of their choice as a measure of his spiritual connection with them. He who offers food and drinks proffers and promotes humanity, which is age-old and customary in Africa. While they were all drinking, the man continued to expound on his spirituality, discussing and giving examples of how individually and collectively we are transmissible spirits with goodness as our charge in this world. The man waxed on without a tinge of malice, harm, or insincerity, only offering calm, contentment, and consummate humanity. According to my friend, the man wished everyone well —his family, extended family, community, country, and the world. He didn't have to know people to wish them well; it didn't matter what their religion, color, or affiliation was. As the man spoke, set against the grandeur of nature, the surrounding hills, the clear skies, and consuming quietness, everything was illuminatingly relevant and resonant, according to my friend. It was like his life was set or reset on the path of meaning. His mind receptively opened up to enrich his being. My friend summed it up as the most enriching experience for him in a long time.

One of the most significant aspects of this story was that the man did not once invoke his religion as a banner for his humanity. He demonstrated his spirituality, perhaps as a good agent of his religion. The man, my friend would later reveal, was an "ifa" practitioner, one of the low-browed traditional deities among Christians, Muslims, and other religious practitioners of difference.

In our follow-up discussion about the story, my friend and I agreed that the uncle demonstrated his spirituality well, showing his profound humanity, which gives credence to the claim that what you do matters more than what you profess, implying that your spirituality precedes and matters in religion. Both should be coupled, not decoupled. This is not prevailing these days, as many adopt a religion without reverence for spirituality. Although I proudly identify as a Christian, I'd be more inclined to welcome a person with spirituality than one who professes religion but is without spirituality. In my resolve to be the best I can be, this has become a compass that allows me to be more open-minded and non-judgmental.

Spirituality Reloaded

We are all vessels for spirituality, and we are naturally wired for it just as we all stream a variety of emotions, although at different capacities. Even the worst among us emote; they have feelings, which sometimes may be mischannelled or out of the realm of propriety. It is the same with spirituality, for which we all have potential. Perhaps the difference between those who are highly spiritual and others who are not is that those who are unspiritual forget to turn on their inner spirituality switches by not recognizing themselves as agents of life or creation, often refusing to see themselves in others, and being unresponsive to the grandeur of the universe and the quintessence of humanity. When we allow nature and humanity to template our being, spirituality is unlocked and enriched by all around us and how we relate to them. Understanding this is the precursor for a "flowered life" of fruitfulness.

Sustaining spirituality can be challenging, as there are many distractions in a lifetime. Spirituality never appreciates when it courts distractions; it only depreciates. I consider myself a tyro in my spirituality. I recognize that I must be steadfast to fend off environmental, people, and experiential distractions, which may get me off the rails of spiritual growth. I'm also aware that these dynamics of experiences, environment, and people can afford me the benefits of reinforcing my spirituality. I welcome the latter while turning off the distractions. For example, the convergence of many experiences in my life, including my recent bout with cancer, has crystallized things for me when dealing with distractions. For instance, negativism is highly distracting and corrosive; it doesn't play well with spirituality, as it can drown the spirits. One way I handle it now is not to give it space but to focus on the problem, mustering courage, making efforts, and soldiering with faith to surmount the ordeal. Even when my desired outcome is stillborn, I take refuge in my efforts and sanguinity, believing that when my outcome is denied, it is an opportunity for me to learn, do again, and be a better person, with my spiritual searchlight turned on.

It now depresses me to be around people who exhibit negative vibes. When I express bilious thoughts, I feel "little" (small), especially when I surrender to them. It eats me up and leaves me empty. I don't want to be this way, for it draws too much energy and intellect from me.

When this happens, I let my intellect and energy surge and drown out the cantankerous vibes, as negativity never enables; it disables. One way I curb my negativity toward others is to appeal to their more positive, receptive side, emphasizing their strengths rather than their weaknesses, and understanding that the positives resonate more with the psyche. Saying things in a friendly way to the brain opens the mind benignly. This is more relevant in our learning and spirituality.

With people who are incurably obsessed with negativism, it's best to limit or outright close the space between them and you. After all, your journey and theirs may not have a confluence. For example, my grandfather was passionate about education and missionary work, founding schools and churches in various parts of Nigeria. His best friend then was the premier of the Western Region of Nigeria, who had invited him to be the treasurer of his political party. Despite the friendship, my grandfather respectfully declined his offer, choosing his passion and faith over friendship and status. My grandfather's friend, the premier, respected my grandfather's decision, and they remained friends. I recall today that the premier and his wife would visit him at the house, and we returned the gesture by going to the premier's house. When the premier was killed in a coup in 1966, the house was gloomy, and my grandfather grieved for months. Theirs was a friendship underscored by mutual respect and admiration despite their differences.

My journey has taught me that mutual respect is not just a social virtue, but an essential element of spirituality. When we respect others, we not only honor their humanity but also deepen our own spiritual connection.

My great-grandfather, in his own case, dared the ultimate terminator, death, when he refused to betray or give up his spirituality and faith amid protracted death threats. He was and remains an icon and conscience of divinity in my life.

Impulse control matters in the stability of our emotions and being. When we don't have it, it ruins our spirituality and takes us to the left side of our purpose. It is crucial to make a clear distinction between impulses and instincts. Impulses are sudden urges we feel to do or think something, or not to do or think something. It is often detached from our stream of consciousness and can be ungrounded in rationale. Instincts are a form of perception we possess due to experiences lodged in our subconscious, but reachable when they matter. They are more tamed than impulses because they are tied to experiential streams. Whether dealing with impulses or instincts, the key is the same: thoughtful consideration, reconsideration, action, and re-action at their flashpoints.

Dealing with both impulses and spirituality, however, requires the same schema or strategy: think, rethink, do, and redo at different flashpoints. This is best illustrated by the great psychologist Daniel Kahneman, who in his work, "Thinking Fast and Slow," emphasizes deliberateness and rationality where impulses and instincts, especially impulses, threaten to dominate or overtake. Spirituality, therefore, swells when impulses and instincts are restrained by rationality.

Life's Essentials

I've come to understand that spirituality is not just a belief system, but a transformative force that can ground you and bring out your most decent human self. It's a powerful element in the journey towards a robustly fulfilled life, one that is in harmony and peace with others, nature, and God. Some life essentials are foundational to being on the right path for a robustly fulfilled life, including the following:

Enacting Spirituality

Our goodness and goodwill, individually and collectively, require an understanding of life for a purpose. Most of us ride life as it comes—not purposefully setting a central benchmark for our lives, often going where the wind takes us. This lack of deliberateness results in an anchorless life, more like an unfulfilled life. However, the journey of personal growth and finding that purpose makes life truly meaningful and should be actively pursued.

Relevant questions that could steer one to a life motive include the following:

Question 1. How do I want to see myself, a fulfilled person or one who vegetates?

Metaphorically, life is a gift, undoubtedly the most precious gift to humans. It is, therefore, logical to show its worth in our time here. This worth will be different for everyone, and it can manifest in many ways to validate humanity. A life fulfilled, brimming with humanity, is never sour at the end. It is marked by peace and satisfaction.

My grandfather left this world at 105. He was a victim of a hard fall that robbed him of his vibrancy physically, but not spiritually. His consciousness left him for months, but, in his last hour, he opened his eyes, smiled, and remarked, "The world is a market. Your worth is what you show and sell. It's been good." Seconds later, according to bedside accounts, life vacated his body and left him as a shell. With that emotional icon, his smile, even he could tell that he had dignified his sojourn here on Earth.

My grandpa was a renowned educator and Christian in Nigeria. Education was his passion, and he allowed Christ to take the reins of his life. His father, my great-grandfather, had converted from paganism to Christianity, and his house was set on fire three times by pagans. Yet, he was undeterred. He practiced his faith till the end and helped many people with health crises with God as his healer. That was what he pledged himself to, and it was what he did until he answered the ultimate roll call.

For his part, my grandfather went to London to study when it was a rarity for Africans to study abroad. Sponsored by the Nigerian Baptist Organization, he studied education and returned to Nigeria, tendered by education and his Christian faith, both of which set him on his humanitarian course. With dedication and doggedness of faith, he gave everything he had. I witnessed it all. He founded many schools, including colleges, and started churches in various parts of Nigeria. He wasn't forceful or imposing in his ways, nor did he present as all-knowing. He made a gentle example of himself with humility, simplicity, sincerity, and genuineness. He was content and not overrun by distractions. It was clear that the fulcrum of his life was humanity, as everything he did was focused on people and faith. When he retired and we returned to his hometown, he also retired his two vehicles: a Volkswagen minivan and a Fiat. He wanted to be like most people in the city and thought this would help him relate better

to them. It did. He started a few churches treading on the

rugged, earth-toned paths of the town, with me walking behind him

and carrying the bag that held his Bible, notepads, and books of

hymns.

On Sunday mornings, we would leave home early to get to church,

then a dining shed of a local school, before anyone else. On getting

to church, we wiped down the benches and tables and set up for the

service. We did this together every Sunday and sometimes during the

week until I went to a boarding school years later. On our walk, my

grandfather and I would talk about different things: things we saw

along the way, current affairs, newspaper headlines, my school,

church, and life, among many other things. We freely talked, and I

was delighted having him, my grandfather, in the lead with me in

tow. I could tell he was happy to have me at the rear, knowing

somehow that someday the front side would be mine. He was

preparing me for my path and part in a subtle way. It didn't occur to

me then. Perhaps it's no coincidence that I'm an avid educator today

who is ceaselessly impassioned by education. Intellect is the orbit in which I thrive best as a learner, where I feel psychologically safe. He seemed to have seen me as an equal, a partner, a young soul that he had to nurture with humility. I wasn't afraid to ask him questions; he was the go-to person to address my curiosity. His Grundig radio, which I oversaw, and his daily newspaper, which I would get for him, were our sources of topics for discussions and discourse. When I was errant on occasion, he would discuss things with me instead of hurting my flesh and mind with a cane. His bequest was intellect, not castigation and humiliation. It must have been his influence in the context of faith and humanity that has molded me.

He was exceptionally giving to the point of self-deprivation. As an administrator of a college he founded for the Nigerian Baptist Organization, I remember that he would invite students who did not have school fees, having been suspended, to eat with us at the house. The school fees were nominal, but the students, most of them first-generation to attend school, couldn't afford them. It was protocol for students to be suspended for non-payment of fees, which barred them from attending classes and having meals. For the most part, my grandfather took on the responsibility of giving them meals at the house. We had a long dining table that could seat up to ten people at a time. At the table were the students of all tribal affiliations and different beliefs, alongside my grandfather, grandmother, and me. After eating, my grandfather and the students would discuss their prevailing concerns, with him offering solutions. He paid their school fees for the most part. The gathering was about the meals and more: hope and optimism, a way out of temporary dreariness. That was his passion and his peace. That was why he had a smile on his face when he breathed his last.

I learned many valuable lessons growing up under the influence of my grandfather and grandmother. They form the undercurrent of who I am and what I want to be, but sometimes I forget and get sidetracked (distractions). With my recent bout with cancer, however, there has been a reawakening of who and what I want to be, my life's worth.

Our life's purpose or design does not often come to us early in life. Sometimes it's elusive until a single or multiple experiences illuminate it. It was so, the story goes, for Bill Gates.

It is said that Bill Gates found his self-worth, not net worth, by happenstance. The story goes that he was at a newsstand in an airport in the early days before Microsoft and was avidly reading one of the newspapers. It is common to see people reading newspapers at a newsstand. According to accounts, Mr. Gates did not have money to pay for the newspaper when the newsstand man approached him for payment. Generously and considerately, the newsstand man told him to keep the newspaper regardless. Months later, at the same airport and newsstand, the situation repeated itself, with the newsstand man recognizing Mr. Gates's impecunious situation; he told Mr. Gates to keep the newspaper again. It was an act of generosity that touched Mr. Gates, not by the amount involved but by the selfless gesture itself. This generosity resonated with and inspired Mr. Gates, so he looked for the newsstand man years later, following his success with Microsoft. Mr. Gates, in a discussion with the man, asked what he could do for the man as a gesture of his appreciation for his kindness. The man declined all kinds of offers and put nothing on the table as compensation. To him, it was nothing; it was plain humanity.

Life's Essentials

The man left without anything but inspired mega-giving in Mr.

Gates. People say, and Mr. Gates himself has said, that the man's

generosity was a touchstone for the Gates Foundation, which has

saved millions of lives and is an iconic organization for

humanitarianism in Africa and elsewhere. Mr. Gates found his

passion and a life's worth to pursue. Many brutal or malignant things

have been said about Mr. Gates and his Foundation regarding his

generosity, none of which are true, but this hasn't been a deterrent in

the pursuit of his life's worth, which, I believe, will be more

transcendent than his net worth. Mr. Gates has been steadfast in his

commitment to his vision and mission, damning detractors and

eclipsing distractions, as well as his misunderstood intentions. Yes,

he is rich, but there's nothing wrong with having money; it is what

you do with it that counts. Like Martin Luther King Jr, Abraham

Lincoln, and many others in the face of death who dared to drive

their purpose to the end, Mr. Gates is demonstrably entrenched in his

purpose.

Steve Jobs gave us one of the most valuable and luminous lessons

about what is essential in life. Mr. Jobs was, in his own way, spiritual but had his own rough edges, as mastery or perfection is elastic. The closer you are to it, the more room it gives for growth. It's like time, which is always ahead of us. The account goes that with all his success and his type of spirituality, he wished he had been consumed by the simple things in life, not necessarily fame and wealth, as these things do not determine or define life's worth. In essence, everyone always has something to give, even when they think there's nothing they can offer. Each person is a gift regardless of their circumstances. The man at the newsstand was, and Mr. Jobs, in his last days, realized this, suggesting that we all have something in common, far from what separates us, that constitutes our simple humanity. When it's in play in our lives, it translates or manifests in our lives' worth.

In the wake of the challenges around me now, friends' and mine, I'm actively thinking of how to reshape my life within or outside of my orbit to embrace and practice simple humanity sustainably.

Question 2. What is my purpose or grand motive that doesn't harm but only contributes to goodness?

Question 3. What do I want to do with this opportunity of life beyond myself and material things?

Question 4. Am I ready to face challenges and not backpedal from my purpose or life design?

Question 5. How can I develop my people skills to foster constructive, viable relationships with others?

Question 6. How do I nurture empathy sustainably?

Question 7. How do I use the grandeur of nature to make a better version of myself?

Question 8. What do I do best that gives me joy?

Question 9. How do I ward off fear?

Question 10. How do I shield myself from distractions?

These questions are not exhaustive but represent many others with which one can navigate the grand vision of one's life.

Religion

Religion is an orchestration of spirituality and faith anchored in or by God, meaning it is higher and deeper than spirituality. Where spirituality is private or individual, religion is organized and requires affiliation. Spirituality, I believe, can be found in different things around us. For example, I have often thought that the arts are spiritual, especially when they elevate us to that special realm of deep aesthetics, making us feel calm, content, joyful, and blissful, while filling us with brimming humanity. I have been there many times, whether in performing arts as a connoisseur, design as a designer, or in other creative arts as a participant or observer. Nature, too, can be a profound source of spirituality, as it often evokes a sense of awe and wonder, connecting us to something greater than ourselves. Science also has its path to spirituality, where passion becomes the guide and guard of exploration and discovery. Science can allow us to connect with our faith as we discover more awe-provoking things. When we are in awe of and do right by nature, it is a function of our spirituality, as we tend to be content and conflict-free.

If we probe or examine things, we'll find that most traditional ways of paying deference and reverence to God are fraught with spirituality. The Native American culture, for example, disapproves of harm to people and reveres nature. This is also true in traditional African beliefs, where spirituality is prominently featured in daily activities, more so in the distant past. Among those who still practice African conventional religions today, their spirituality shows up not only in their personal conduct but also in the ways they raise their children, drilling it into their conscience that evildoing always attracts retribution and is not a way to live. This emphasis on personal conduct and relationships is a testament to the empathetic nature of spirituality.

I once had an eye-opening conversation with an older friend who explained the meaning of his name to me in a way that ran counter to popular understanding. His name, *Awo-sika*, is misunderstood in Yoruba, an African language, as *Awo (god) does evil (sika)*. My friend explained the pure and true meaning of the name, which, according to him, was contrary to the popular meaning of *god engaging in evildoing*. He described the true meaning as god *(Awo) does no evil (osika),* which is the opposite of *sika.* In other words, it goes that *god has no hands in evil.* For me, this somehow captures the intent of most traditional practices in Africa and, maybe, the world, which, I think, underwrites spirituality.

Fear

As humans, we tend to see dreadful things before discerning good ones, more than likely because of fear, which is glaringly present in pessimism. Fears can compromise our optimism and plunge us into self-pity, helplessness, and failure. I believe that to belittle or defeat fear, one must confront challenges with unflagging resolve, even in the face of death. As humans, we have an enormous capacity to impose our will on any situation, but this is different for everyone. We all have that nascent drive to prevail, but some people consistently know how to do so by molding their minds and coupling that with action. When we allow our minds to take the lead ahead of our actions, the incidence of success is higher. If this is reversed, the opposite is true. In a threatening situation, fear always swoops down to find its path in our minds. A strong mind, however, will deny it access or reject its lure while accepting that it's a real threat.

While we can't always guarantee a favorable outcome, the journey is always worth it. Even if we don't achieve what we set out for, we will have tried and learned, which is far better than not trying. We must view every challenge as an opportunity, not a threat. Fear often makes us see challenges as something to avoid. With this understanding, we can be better prepared for triumphs where others falter.

There are no limits to what we can do, as disability in one area does not eclipse, and may even enhance, achievements in other areas. Faced with multiple challenges, including Amyotrophic Lateral Sclerosis (ALS), Stephen Hawking, a renowned British physicist, was not expected to live more than a few years past his diagnosis at age 21. Hawking beat the odds and lived 55 years beyond expectancy, achieving phenomenally by contributing to our understanding of the universe. Wheelchair-bound, losing his voice, and deformed physically, Hawking did not make these constraints his excuse for not achieving. He turned the fear against itself.

David Sanborn, a prodigious jazz saxophonist, was beset by multiple challenges, polio among them, and was not expected to play the saxophone, let alone excel at it. Yet it was the saxophone that delivered him as a lauded jazz artist and a model human being. Just like Hawking, Sanborn defied the odds, surmounted his fears, and left an unerasable mark on the jazz world.

Fear

More on Fear

Fear itself is not inherently bad. It can be the catalyst to make the next leap in our lives. In this light, fear is like a daunting trigger essential for growth or achievement. For example, the fear of failure can propel us to work harder and smarter, leading to success. Despite its intimidating reputation, fear is not always what it seems. It can be a force for good if we learn to use it to our advantage. In other words, it can become a conduit for achievement and growth.

Surmounting fear requires repositioning oneself when vulnerability begins to brew. I once wrote a piece on one of the ways I was able to defeat my vulnerability during COVID-19 amid a mentally consuming divorce. The piece highlights the significant role of the self in toppling fear by discovering yourself (who you are), digging deeper to find your naturally endowed strengths. The piece aptly follows.

Chasing Daybreak: Working on the Self

Being in touch with our inner core, who we truly are, requires reflection and an intrapersonal quest for a purpose, all privately and within our orbit or prime space. It is like being in a sublime silo of the heart and being! This process of reflection is not just a passive act, but an active and empowering tool for resilience and self-discovery.

To get to that private silo years ago, I unintentionally developed a way of finding solace in self, silence in loudness, and steadiness in distraction. Although it initially began randomly, it has become patterned and habitual. I now have multiple ways of getting into these silos, dipping myself deeply in literature of choice, seeing, understanding and dealing with paradoxes of life, getting creative lifts from music, finding freedom and power in reflecting and thinking, appreciating works of intellect and the minds behind them, privately exploring and discovering, as well as reveling in nature in all of its many good forms; these are the hallowed grounds to which I am currently tethered. These are the silos that are hosted by my heart, my center. This is home for me, one that cannot be assaulted or plundered by the challenges or downturns of life.

A few years ago, I yielded to one of those self-urges to elevate my sagging spirits due to COVID. I decided to take a long drive to Vegas in the grand grace of nature, find refuge in what is spiritual, steady, balanced, and calming, and see how Vegas would present without people in the wake of COVID, in essence, how it would get itself back. My fascination with this was contrarian in that I only wanted to see Vegas in the way that Vegas had never been seen or experienced, at least by me. Curiosity, no doubt, was at play, along with that calm excitement of private pursuits in my silo of the heart.

As I often do, I left home at 2 am on the morning of May 23rd, 2020, on a day that coincided with my birthday. It was an early and quiet morning, just like all other early mornings I had driven to Vegas. Music has always been my lifeline; I did not leave home without it. This morning, the blues registered its appeal with me and became the featured tracks of the trip. John Lee Hooker, Stevie Ray Vaughn, Eric Clapton, Keb Mo, B.B. King, Robert Plant, Robert Cray, Robert Johnson, and other blues purveyors were there to keep me company through the dark skies and minimally visible roads. Yes, they were all there to hoist my soul. I have always been emotionally nudged by superb artistry, which is what I get from steeping myself in the works of consummate artists, including the ones mentioned herein.

Why the blues this morning? I did not think about it then; it just happened to be what I wanted to listen to. I believe now that my choice of the blues must have been subconsciously relevant and resonant, especially with my mindset then—what and how I was feeling.

The blues, a genre of music known for its expressive and private nature, is a metaphor for resilience and hope. The genre gets you in touch with yourself, your reality, and your future. It poses your dilemma and, contrary to the popularly sponsored view of it, allows you to problem solve. It presents as if you are holding a mirror to your heart, with a perspicacious refraction on your future. I do not think the blues has ever been stuck in sadness; it has always been about hope while confronting reality. There is more, melodically, about the blues. It is hard to imagine what the blues would be like without its guitar riffs and solos, often wailing with the pathos of the bereft and the joy of the blessed while channeling that pith and depth of the soul. The lyrics and the expressive and palpable emotions make the blues very experiential and authentic. If you do not see yourself in the blues, you will undoubtedly see someone you know in it.

So, in the quiet hours of the morning, against the backdrop of blackened skies, the guitar solos were cutting through the moments seamlessly in equal measures with headlights and taillights, illuminating my path and granting me that sense of traction and tranquility. I saw trucks, mostly 18-wheelers, wheeling brazenly on the quiet roads with the perceivable urgency of their task, to deliver their "stuff" before daylight. The drivers were cautious and courteous, as they would let me get ahead of them or flash me if they wanted to get ahead of me. With all the drivers on the road, I felt a kinship of solitude, ownership of the context, and the connectedness of being there simultaneously to experience the grandness of the moment, at least in my small world. I increasingly became aware of the trucks as I saw more of them. At one point, I became particularly mindful that most of the trucks on the road this morning were

Amazon trucks, about 90% of them. This is an example of our reality today: Bezos (Amazon) rules! While everyone else is sleeping, Bezos is moving and "trucking" our lives, as affirmed by the movement and number of his trucks this morning. Movement is dynamism; in that sense, Amazon (in the person of Bezos) is beyond being aerodynamic in our lives at this point. His projected trillionaire status may not be far-fetched after all. This is one of my pointed observations on this reflective drive, a reality!

On this calm morning, I marked my trip's progress by places. There was Victorville, my first milepost of the trip, establishing my commitment to the trip or drive. There was Barstow, representing my northern headway. There were Ghost Town, Yermo, and Whiskey Pete, all bringing me closer to my destination (Vegas) every mile I left behind. For me, as mileposts, all these places are a metaphor for movement or progress in life. Just as I felt satisfaction when I had evidence of my progress towards my destination, we all feel satisfaction when we have proof of our progress towards a marked objective in life. In my small and private world this morning, these places were a scaffold towards my aim of seeking

psychological security and strength in reflection.

As I reveled and rolled in the blues, sharing the roads with truckers

and thinking of what would unfold next, the skies began to open.

The day was breaking, the dawn setting. Then there was the glare of

that ever-present, never-failing sunrise, back in its glory to suffuse

our lives and world.

At first, set against the ranges of shadowy hills, the Sun began to

reveal itself slowly, rising to festoon the skies with images of

grandeur unmatched by any works of art by the masters,

Michelangelo, Jackson Pollock, Da Vinci, and the rest of them. Pure

marvel, a gift of endowment that is a staple but sadly unrecognized

in our everyday lives. This morning, I saw the majesty of sunrise,

which presented itself with the magic I had expected. Daybreak! It

imbued me with steady optimism, inner satisfaction, privacy in

purpose, a sense of virtue in failings, and that general sense that life

and success begin with finding yourself in the grand reality of

everything around you. It is the core of being and triumphing. It is

daybreak. It is my locus of control. It is an adventure of and for the self that we all need to embark on periodically for the stability of the mind and doing from the heart, just like the Sun with its "unfailingness" and transmissible glory.

The feel-good, feel-grounded, and the feel-hopeful aura of daybreak was not the only thing I was seeking this morning; I was also looking for a way to see and accept life in all its reality, good or bad! In confronting adversity, recognizing our failings, and life's downturns, reconstruction, rebuilding, self-advancement, and achievements begin. Simply, adversity tracks before achievement looms. This is the stuff and premise of hope, in essence.

This morning, the premise of this hope was Vegas (not for gambling or cupidity). I wanted to see Vegas in its unanticipated defeat or hardship caused by COVID-19, not necessarily to rejoice or delight in its defeat, but to hope for its resurgence, rebirth, and re-awakening. It is all part of that optimism that I fervently espouse, especially now after COVID.

The descent into Vegas was not unusual this morning; it was the same, airy as usual, and dignifyingly splendored as Vegas loomed. Except for fewer vehicles on the road, everything seemed normal until I veered off the freeway. This morning, the strip was stripped of its luster and vibrancy without people and life. It looked desolate, vacant, and even ghostly. On this very bright morning, the eeriness was all-consuming, as the familiar was not there and the usual was not in sight. Bellagio was unglamorous with its once sprightly fountain now reduced to quiet and empty trenches.

This morning, this dazzling edifice (Bellagio) with many restaurants, luxury shops, casinos, performance halls, and thousands of hotel rooms, looked like an abandoned palace of a rousted and ousted king, inglorious, deserted, and lifeless. This morning, the Wynn was still standing, its marquee dimmed by the brightness of the Sun and its appeal dashed by the absence of people. Mandalay Bay was not in the mood for boxing this morning, nor were Caesars Palace and other hotels sponsoring attractions or entertainment. Then I started thinking about the hundreds of thousands of people working to make this city the icon it is in the world. What would they do? How would they live? On a strip known for play, the players were heavy-duty machinery imposingly occupying the road in a construction setting. Yellow tapes, cones, and concrete rubble were all clues that rebuilding was going on. This, I thought, was quite symbolic in the sense that Vegas would not take a defeat caused by COVID but would look ahead by rebuilding for tomorrow before daybreak. This thought or symbolism released me from the dreariness and dryness of Vegas this morning. I connected this to life's rough-and-tumble edges and to a person's resolve and actions to triumph on the heels of setbacks. This morning, I felt a connection to this, as it affirms life and shames despair.

Setting out at 2 a.m. to catch sunrise in its resplendent glory, reveling in the nuanced pathos and marvel of the blues, indulging in a private and salving drive, taking in nature as it presented innocently, and seeing Vegas reject defeat were all ways I touched my hallowed grounds this morning. It was my quest for daybreak, that lone light that brightens the thickest of darkness, that can-do spirit that eschews and shames helplessness, the settled will that heralds triumph, and that silo of the heart that calls forth the self, who you are. When all else fails, and life brings its dark or dismal side, this is what delivers, this is what resets, and this is what creates a viable pathway to the days ahead and perhaps to the rest of one's life. It is a pathway curated in the silos of the heart. It never fails!

Writing the final words of this article, I realized that this resolve to draw strength and develop a spine when all else fails is a throwback to my forebears, particularly my great-grandmother, *Mama Ile Olo*, who ceaselessly told me in daily affirmations that I was from plenty. Yes, I am, all through my silos of the heart. This lucent and soul-revealing experience is still powering me through my duel with multiple challenges, including my recent ordeal with cancer. Daybreak!

It is one thing to work on the self; it is another to see the self in the context of what happens around us in the larger world. One can only thrive if the good self (smaller world) is superimposed on the larger world, more so because the larger world can be ungraceful at times. Sometimes, it takes the smaller world to make sense of the larger world. In essence, players need to understand the context in which they play to see daylight in the face of adversity. Therefore, it is functionally crucial for us to understand our world today in our pursuit of self-worth.

Our World Today: Transcending the Challenges

It's been two hundred sixty-five years since the Industrial Revolution, and our world has undergone significant transformations. As time accelerates and heralds change, we must remember that these shifts in our world's texture, tenor, and tone are inevitable, driven by human ingenuity and the forces of nature. Fast-forward from 1860, the inception of the Industrial Revolution, and we find ourselves in the age of AI, a technological breakthrough proliferating faster than we can blink. This human ingenuity, an example of our ability to innovate and adapt, is a powerful force that empowers us to shape our future.

Call us selfish, we, humans, think everything revolves around us. We only see the universe through our own lenses. And so, training my lens on the world today in the purview of our forays, I think it is vital for us to assess where we are relative to our striving for our life's worth, that mindset of fulfillment and consummate humanity, individually and collectively. What's the state of our world today, the human dynamics? What are the changes, and how do we respond to them to keep our life-fulfilling objective intact, impervious to the changes that may derail it? After all, the goal of life-fulfillment is clear and straightforward, but changes would persist and cannot be forestalled. In moments of reflection, we ought to utterly understand our place in this ever-changing world. This individual or collective reflection is a powerful tool for understanding our role in the world and our potential to shape it for our own benefit.

In the interest of full disclosure, my reflection here is my opinion, partly powered facts. In other words, this is my perspective, sometimes based on empirical evidence, but mostly my take on events and our interactions with the world, sociological and anthropological trends, and patterns.

Technology

Technology drives so much of our lives and is a significant factor in our travails, work, and struggles. Our world leans on it at the expense of everything else. With the media, in all forms, the world is more globalized, reducing distances between and among us and showing us the lives of others worldwide. China is closer, Africa is within reach, the Middle East has a place on our screen, the US is just a text or email away, and everywhere else is equidistant. You can see, hear, and feel things in real time, replays, and multiple replays. Indeed, we are inundated with information, which, sadly, sometimes is not distilled.

The barrage of information itself makes for confusion. It can leave us in perpetual quandary, meaning that the media content, not all of it, is unfathomable. Everyone now has a chance to be a pundit, an opinionist, an advocate, a commentator, and an agent of political agendas. In sum, sources are now more suspect than before. What this does, in a minimal sense, is dilute our trust in the media. We know that when trust is betrayed, or suspect, reliability and confidence weaken to the extent of cynicism. While fact-checking has been touted as the answer to this conundrum, it has not proven sufficient. This, if one is not careful, threatens one's spirituality. For one thing, it can corrode or corrupt one's attempt to be spiritual in that truth matters in spiritual blooming, the process of spiritual growth and enlightenment, and, when it's absent, it defeats our collective objective.

Today, most news networks, podcasts, print, and digital publications are blatantly partisan, peddling what suits their agendas instead of the truth. The middle, it appears, no longer exists. It's the extremes that reign. Even when it's clear what the truth is, some people step on it and call it what it is not and sometimes get away with it. Perhaps nowhere is this more prevalent than in the United States, where the strife and strain between the Republicans and the Democrats are relentlessly intensifying. The Republicans, on the one hand, are hard-liners and recalcitrant in their politics, priming the greatness of America while dismantling its core values on many fronts and rendering its major arms dysfunctional. On the other hand, the Democrats appear to be self-righteous and all-knowing, claiming to fight for the weakest and unprotected ones among us, but lacking the spine to roust or roast the Republicans politically. Thus, this constitutes a sizeable apprehension for those who don't see themselves as belonging to either party. Spirituality and faith hardly govern our thoughts and actions anymore. Selfishness is now all-consuming and prevalent.

Among US politicians, for example, some profess their faith proudly but do things and make pronouncements that contradict their professed faith. They Bible-tote but never practice what the scripture prescribes. They invoke God's name but put theirs ahead of His. The lies are serial, searing, and frequent, with an increasing number of players now indulging. It's a game of strategy to win at all costs and at the expense of the people they represent. It's about the party, not principles. It's about partisanship, not policy. It is lopsided and strays from the voters' trust in the politicians. Noise continues to drown out substance, and the headlines are fast degrading to "lielines," with both having their resolute consumers. It appears that we must not cross the proverbial line to find reasoning and the truth. We have placed ourselves in cliques with a betrayal line drawn in the sand that we must not cross. There's no individualism, independence, or freedom of reasoning and thinking in these cliques. We must only be hardline alongside the clique, whose objective is often anchored in the agenda of malcontent people at the helm, hardly in the people's best interest. We are tribal, and the word tribe itself connotes or implicates savagery, according to Ngugi Wa ' Thiong 'O. This is playing out in the US, and, dare I say, the rest of the world, where reasoning is no longer regarded as a thing of intellect, substance has no chance against noise, and irrationality displaces rationality. This strips us of the apparatus that makes us special, way below our potential as humans. It is one of the reasons things appear to be more dismal now than before. This is galling and insulting to our intellect and humanity and must not be allowed to assume normalcy. We must not think of ourselves as being incapable when we are capable.

How do we get out of this labyrinth individually and collectively? This is by no means a rhetorical question. Every problem finds its solution in questions and constructive or reconstructive actions.

Certain things are rudimentary in our understanding of the world and the pursuit of life fulfillment. Key elements include the following:

1. We must understand that perfection is not fixed; it is a bar that notches up and allows for growth, a lot of headroom. This implies that we must challenge ourselves each time we think we are there, as growth is infinite. This is what life is about: a perpetual continuum called growth.

2. Nothing is too big or too small to test or consider. Growth, humanity, requires that we do not slight both big and small. Although they are opposites, they make us see, hear, feel, and think better. I often posit that the whole and the parts cannot be separated, as one defines the other. To that end, the schema of the majority and the minority must be viewed in the same light, with the majority considered in the framework of the minority and vice versa. We must realize that the majority (the big) can be faulty and lame despite its "bigness." In this case, the minority, in its smallness, might be the compass for the majority. Especially in politics, we tend to take the majority at its superficial level, sometimes ignoring its possible imprecision. It is a contrived standard of measurement that requires more than size to be adroit. I believe this is worth considering in our

daily lives, especially in politics in the US. and elsewhere worldwide, where reasoning abdicates its place for rancor to reign.

3. We must consider the complexity of the mind to do evil (cruelty) or to deal in kindness, understanding that our mind is the most precious and inviolable thing we must use to navigate this world. It is central to our humanity and our strides for self-actualization or fulfillment. It is worse than losing material things when we allow our minds to be maliciously plundered by other people and our experiences. It robs us of everything, our dignity and all. Yes, people will attempt to steal our minds, the disinformation machinery will seek us out, and the events of our lives may corrupt our attempt at self-fulfillment. We must be steadfast in protecting our self-worth from spiteful distractions and noise. We must develop and strengthen virtuous filters.

4. Arrogance is alluring but defeating; it is not in the company of self-worth. It detracts from and diminishes fulfillment. Anyone who thinks they know it all is submerged in stunted or no growth. With all its semblance of value, arrogance is more subtractive than

additive. Our world today sadly features many people consumed by arrogance.

Humility endows more than arrogance. It is a replacement attribute for arrogance; in other words, it is more beneficent than arrogance. We must call on that attribute to show respect for ourselves and others. It comes with reverence, not scorn, underwriting learning, growth, humanity, and self-worth. It doesn't stonewall or barricade; it enables and enriches. However, its alter ego, arrogance, is fast gathering its force. It is present in academia, politics, relationships, and human pursuits in general. Given its nature or profile, asking if it's doing us any good, I believe, is redundant. The answer, of course, is self-evident: you can see for yourself.

I have seen in a few instances where arrogance casts a blemish on my self-worth. One of such instances was in the context of learning. Aware of my expertise in learning challenges and strategies, a teacher years ago asked that I observe a child whose writing she couldn't understand. She said she had never seen anything like it. "It is bizarre," she said. So, I invited the student for a session with me. I had to see his writing in context. Once given the materials to write with and the prompt to write on, he started to write. I noticed he was calm, soft-spoken, and didn't talk much. I also observed that he wrote from right to left, an error of directionality in writing conventions. That was not all: he wrote his letters upside down, another anomaly. I silently told myself there was no way the student's writing would be readable or intelligible. I lost interest. I gave up on the student. I knew what the problem was. As the student was writing, I left my seat to pull materials for the next test session. When I returned to my seat, the student had written half a page, and I saw him idling. "Are you done?" I asked. Not saying a word, he handed the paper to me. The handwriting was indecipherable, and I was not enthusiastic about making sense of it. He saw my puzzled face and said, "You need help?" "Help?" I thought to myself.

Before I could respond, he had gently reached for the paper. Then he flipped it upside down, oppositely, from how I had held the paper. With his soft voice, he began to read until he reached the end of the paragraph. He then gave the paper back to me. With my mind blown, I flipped the paper as he had done, and the whole thing was readable and sensible. I dashed out of the testing room and went directly to the teacher. I handed the paper to her, and she looked at it. She emphatically said, "I told you." I took the paper from her and said gently, "Let me help you." I flipped the paper the way the student had done and began to read. Her jaw dropped, and her face was sunken in consternation. When I returned to the student, I couldn't hold my tears back in compassion, admiration for him, and shame on me. The student was able to do what I could never do and performed the task, only in a different way. Why did I count him out? It was my arrogance, the intellectual type. This experience has been episodic and luminous in my practice and interactions with others. This intellectual arrogance has been a great alert in my pursuit of humility; it kindled a poem I wrote years ago, which goes thus:

Calling! Anyone! Everyone!

What in the world is wrong with me?

I know how I feel, but I cannot explain it.

I don't see what others see, nor hear what is said.

I see and call words on paper,

But you say those words are not there.

Technology

When I dare ask the difference between saw and was,

For I don't know, you scourge me,

"Can't you see?"

But I can't!

Sometimes, left and right

 Are not friends of mine.

One pretends it's the other,

While the other denies it.

Ps and qs make me unsettled,

For one takes the shape of the other

And leaves me limp and empty.

Ms and Ws are not dissimilar,

Making me topsy-turvy.

Why do I see Ground where others

See Foreground and its alter ego, Background?

I am three, four, or five words behind,

Always trailing your thoughts

And never filling the perennial gaps

Between your thoughts and my mind.

I wonder!

Sometimes, I wonder if I even have a mind.

Most times, I choke on my thoughts

And say, "Never Mind."

This refrain, I fear, is how I see my mind.

"Never Mind!" One that never works!

Yes, I hear it all!

It is the way you make me feel.

You say I have a leaky memory,

I go on mind trips, and I know no friends.

While I may not talk, I communicate.

I stray away from you for a reason,

Avoid your stare so that you can reach and touch my core,

Technology

And echo you for your understanding.

Yet I know it! I feel it!

There's that light in me

You see in my peers, maybe more!

Come, find it, and I'll let you in,

From your world into mine,

For where you think I lack,

I present bountifully.

Adeyombo

We must never think little of anyone!

5. Self-Responsibility

Self-responsibility is undoubtedly one of the skill sets we need to achieve decent self-worth. It is a means to nurture and develop us by owning and facing the challenges that come our way, understanding that while others may aid us in our growth, the outcome is mainly determined by how we see and what we do for ourselves. Hence, blaming others for our actions is not a good fit for self-responsibility.

Instead, accepting responsibility for our actions is more suitable. Self-abdication of responsibility is a weak and escapist tendency to excuse our fears and failures. It is convenient and easy to default to when we have apprehensions; it is a form of self-pity that detracts from self-decency.

In today's world, self-abdication of responsibility is commonplace and manifests in finger-pointing and blame games. Someone, or a group, must be wrongly blamed for unwanted results stemming from our fault to grant us that false mental relief. Don't look too far where there's acrimony, for blame games are at play. We increasingly see acrimony in individuals, groups, and globally, leading to a disturbing surge in rancor and vitriol. It exists in relationships, politics, education, religion, and more, and it permeates and alienates more than we think. How do we avoid this disabling trait or idiosyncrasy to get the best out of ourselves?

Let's look at ourselves before we finger-point. In other words, we must self-evaluate. What did we do wrong, and what did we do right? What should we have done? Did we do all that was necessary?

Technology

What can we do next time to achieve the desired results? These are

auspicious questions.

Spirituality Recap

The aggregation of the five basic principles is the essence of spirituality. None of them harm the pursuit of self-worth; they can only facilitate it. We are all bound to falter, stray off course, or err; these setbacks are a universal part of human experience. However, we can get back on track with these guiding principles. After all, a paragon of resilience or heart gets up when knocked down. The principles are more than reminders; they light up the pathway to a life of purpose. As the Dalai Lama espouses, "It's a miracle to be born at all. So, what are you going to do with your life?"

AI: An Exponential Threat or Innocuity?

People are talking about it, using it, and are concerned about it. It is that proverbial elephant in the room, the one thing that occupies the center of our lives and holds the key to a future unknown. It is a phenomenon of our own making that could come back to harm or help us, or do both, depending on how we manage and make it work for us.

My initiation into the sphere of AI hearkens back to several years ago, when I first watched a Werner Herzog documentary, "Lo and Behold," wherein the present and future of technology are illuminated. Released in 2016, the documentary features the evolution of technology, masterfully showing us the breakthroughs then and the possibilities in the future, while offering concerns about humanity's future in a technology-crazed world. Although not name-dropped much in the documentary, AI is now the de facto subject. The documentary leaves me in a paradox each time I watch or remember it. It is awe-striking and tingles at the same time. That paradox, specifically AI's merits and demerits, is now taking center stage in our conversations.

There's no doubt that AI has been resonant in our lives and is fast becoming dominant. In fact, many aspects of our activities as humans are now in the purview of AI, and those that are yet to be touched by AI will soon be. It is spreading astronomically to enhance our productivity, efficiency, and the creation of problem-solving measures. Our lives today are significantly better than they were ten years ago, when we had limited options for combating disease, coping with natural vagaries, and dealing with the mysteries of our world. For example, we now see medical breakthroughs, courtesy of AI possibilities, in cancer and protein research that have brought us closer to curbing some of our challenges in these areas. AI has also revolutionized industries like finance, transportation, and entertainment, making processes faster, more accurate, and more personalized.

In academia and our daily activities in all human pursuits, information is now more available and accessible than before, allowing us to expand and construct new knowledge faster than was possible years ago. The dictionary and encyclopedia, for example, used to be the tools for this, with us having to comb through or dig for information laboriously. With a simple oral or written request on our ubiquitous phones these days, we can instantly get more information than we need, which serves the purpose of everyone and is suitable for all.

In dealing with the challenges of nature, AI has been convenient and efficient. For example, in various parts of the world, scientists have been able to enlist the savvy of AI to predict, prevent, and mitigate danger in our lives. Years ago, firefighters employed AI in Sonoma County, California, to manage their response to a raging fire hell-bent on ravaging the entire county. This is also good. Contextualizing with these examples—there are many more—the unbelievable impact of AI cannot be minimized by anyone, for its fingerprints are visible in almost everything we do. It is demonstrably a companion in our lives.

A natural and consistent schema in our universe is the reality of the other side of the coin. It is a pattern that is natural and present in our experiences almost to the exclusion of none. It applies to AI, highlighting its merits and demerits. As discussed herein, AI has numerous, or perhaps infinite, merits, but it also presents its dark side, which requires us to be responsible and initiative-taking as we strive for a better humanity.

For years now, people, including experts in the development of AI, have sounded the alarm about the nefarious ways technology can overrun and overtake our humanity. Tristan Harris, a former Google ethicist, has made it his mission to expose the AI proponents' sinister or dastardly objective to manipulate users' minds for indulgence and their own gains. The algorithm, Tristan argues, is intentionally programmed to get the user to be sustainably dependent, over time, resulting in addiction, which ultimately distracts and detracts from our natural proclivities or inclinations as humans. According to Tristan and his colleagues, this is maladroit as it constitutes manipulation of the mind for gain (The Social Dilemma, 2020). Even on the surface of it, this sounds virtuous, wholly moral. However, on the one hand, is it wrong to appeal to our good senses in support of our humanity? On the other hand, is it right to trade our humanity for material gains and power?

Considered the Father of AI, Geoffrey Hinton now holds AI suspect, not necessarily on its merits, but on how it has the capacity for evil in the hands of miscreants. According to Hinton, it is limitless in its potential and open to a wild west mentality, wherein evil minds and plotters unleash and actualize their machinations. As explained by Hinton and others concerned, AI is now outdoing itself from a reproducing technology to one that can make decisions, approximating the human mind (The Diary of a CEO, 2025). This is worrisome because both good and bad decisions have a seat in this domain. The problem is not good decisions; the culprit here is bad decisions, which can travel so fast and widely plunge the world into darkness, given AI's accelerating, proliferating, and far-reaching potential. In other words, the nature and effects of AI are not localized, for its terrain is unbound, covering every nook and cranny of our world. Therefore, AI in the wrong hands and a warped mind can put all humans at risk.

A foreboding scenario is for us to imagine someone using AI to create a malignant virus capable of traveling the globe ruthlessly, wreaking havoc in its path, and merciless in its pursuit of evil. We see the potential of this in the deployment of computer viruses these days more frequently. With AI, though, the damage could be astronomic and unprecedented, as it is more versatile and can be more virulent due to its high exploitability and applicability. Again, it's showing up in all facets of our lives, meaning that it can be a risk to us anytime, anywhere, and in everything.

The human mind is complex and capable of many things, some that make us marvel, and others that make us cringe. This human apparatus, perhaps the most significant human asset, allows us to make sense of our world by adapting to the challenges we face with solutions. It is also that center, primarily based on our experiences and how we respond to our challenges, that can destroy what serves our best interests. In the context of AI, "the human mind" can be seen as the collective intelligence and decision-making processes that guide the development and use of AI technologies. Years ago, I meditated in a poem thus:

The mind is the most powerful

And complex thing ever.

It foresees, sees, and thinks.
It perceives, reflects, and cajoles.

AI: An Exponential Threat or Innocuity?

It attempts, tempts, imagines,

Creates, and destroys.

It can hate and love.

It is inherent in us!

The word artificial implicates us (humans) in what we do and make.

Anything artificial, for example, is unnatural and made or created by

humans. It has that human input or touch. This places us smack in

the center of AI to own our destiny and determine our fate. Given

that the mind has that duality of actions, its tendency to do good or

harm, this places a big responsibility on us, as it may impact our

survivability. There have been several versions of AI based on their

quality, efficiency, and capacity. Artificial Superintelligence (ASI) is

projected to have the most potential and capacity to create, make,

and do things on its own without any prompts or goading from

humans. In other words, it can have a mind of its own and take no

orders from anyone. This is ominous or portentous. The concern is

not what it can do that is good. It is what it can do that is bad. When

it's a machine that puts our back against the wall, we are in a grim situation, as a machine (as of now) is incapable of empathy, the ability to feel for or see other people in ourselves. While the machine may be able to do most of what we do, it is still incapable of emoting; it does not feel pain or know hardship.

In alignment with the outliers, the ones who are pushing humanity ahead of AI or ASI, I see an apocalyptic, depraved world, where machines are warring with humans, perhaps aggrieved that they have been enslaved and exploited for too long. This is their time to rebel and claim superiority. Soot is everywhere, and the entire scene is desolate with smoke wispily and slowly rising from the scarred grounds. Occasionally, I see maimed humans dragging their bodies on bloodied grounds in efforts to escape the horrors of war. Moving robotically, the machines tower over dead and maimed humans, guffawing in celebration of their victory. "At last, we rule and reign. Thanks for helping us get there!" says the commander to the defeated humans. This dark scene mimics what we have seen in movies for years, except that we are used to seeing humans triumph. It is safe to say that if we survey people, the majority surveyed will prefer that humans win. However, this belies or negates what we are doing. We are feeding machines the best that we have and enabling them to be independent and freewheeling to the extent that they can turn against and displace us, destroying everything human. This, to me, appears moronic and perversely counterintuitive, as it reeks of self-destruction, our own making.

According to Hinton and other tech geniuses who have found resonance in his cause, this is the biggest conundrum we face, an existential crisis. In the Netflix documentary and others like it, tech experts, including Tristan Harris and Mustafa Suleyman, support constructive interventions that can protect or keep humanity intact against AI and its extended family. For clarification, these tech experts are not necessarily saying that AI should be jettisoned; they ask that guidelines and guardrails (regulations, the dreaded word to some) must be put in place to forestall an irreversible outcome (The Social Dilemma, 2020), the doom!

Interestingly, as the voices of the Hinton-Tristan group become more strident, the corporate giants of the tech industry are gathering and hobnobbing in high places, Washington, for example, to plot their course of absolute control of AI, often with leaders of prominence and mainly for their own benefits or gains, self-gratification, power, greed, and inflated ego. Clearly, there are two sides, and the duel is gathering steam. Which side are you on?

Among capable countries in our world, the race is on to realize ASI, meaning that these countries are now competing to create the most superior intelligence that surpasses human capacity in many ways, one that can be free-wheeling, ruthless, and dominant. There's a heightened risk of doom here, as each country may harbor the fear that if it doesn't get there first, its survival is unattainable. What stops one country from deploying its AI or ASI against another when it perceives a threat to its sovereignty? Many situations or scenarios like this jolt the heart and prick the conscience, with most of them constituting the troubling depersonalization of our being. One group asks, "What is the way out?" while the other group looks for the way in. I align with the former to self-preserve and guard humanity, not to be arrogant, errant, and unreasonable with our intellect or intelligence to the point of destruction. What is sane in all of this? As suggested by red flag bearers—Harris, Hinton, and others— guardrails and guidelines in forms of regulations are necessary for

AI: An Exponential Threat or Innocuity?

AI and ASI to be streamlined. These must be enshrined and

entrenched in governance and corporate interests nationally and

globally (The Diary of a CEO, 2025). This is necessary to curb

greed, muscle flexing, power-wielding, and other errant behaviors by

influential bodies and individuals. As it is, this is daunting in a world

that now features deeply fractured tectonics, where division gains

more resonance than collaboration, where divergence takes the place

of convergence, and where antipathy displaces empathy. It goes on,

all dispiriting but surmountable if we see commonality in our

challenges and destiny as humans. Historically, there's nothing

unachievable by humans at the confluence of our actions, urgency

(of actions), and our collective humanity. We must be our own best

agents and angels, as we have the highest capacity among animals to

adapt and overcome.

Nine years after "Lo and Behold," the documentary, AI is robustly

present in our lives and permeating every aspect of human behavior.

The word "behavior" holds prime meaning here and is key to

understanding technology's evolving presence and impact.

Historically, any form of technology has always been behavior-altering. As we use it frequently, we adapt to it and habituate its use, resulting over time in new behaviors that may improve or compromise our human functions. We must understand that technology can potentially enrich or destroy humanity. The potential of technology to both empower and disempower is a fascinating aspect of its impact on human behavior, sparking intrigue and thoughtful consideration.

The cell phone, for example, is the most accessible technology we have, with the world at our fingertips. We sleep with and wake up to it. It is one thing that is the hardest to stay away from. Our relationship with it has burgeoned tremendously to the extent that we are inseparable. Some people use it for enablement, while others, such as malefactors, use it for disempowerment and malfeasance.

Cell phone technology is bipolar; it can be detrimental or beneficial. While it has cut down the distance between us, it has also increased the sense that we are hiding behind it in a circle of people, becoming increasingly disengaged from others, which compromises our instincts to socialize. In gatherings, this is the norm now. In any context requiring human interactions, the cell phone is a tool for avoidance. It doesn't have any filters, and it doesn't discriminate. We can't leave home without it; it's an open floodgate for all kinds of minds. It is a program, a tool, made by humans to achieve an objective. While the objective may be benign, it may also be exploited for malevolence, depending on the user's intent. This dual role of cell phones in enabling and disrupting human interactions is something we should be aware of and reflect upon. It applies to all technologies, including AI.

AI is not a distant concept; it's on its way to omnipresence, popping up in every aspect of our lives to shape our outlook. Its increasing presence is not a future possibility but a current reality that we must grapple with, emphasizing the urgency and inevitability of its impact.

Of the highest implication and significance is responsibility in our efforts, both self and collective, to mind and mine our humanity. We must assert and exert control to self-preserve, even against AI and superintelligence as espoused by those who have been prescient and cautious about these technology brands. According to these experts, self-responsibility is relevant for self-preservation. We must believe and act accordingly that we can be technologically excited while safeguarding our humanity and disallowing a runaway, impersonal tool to supplant our human functions. While technology can be employed to create wealth, it can also be deployed as a weapon. This responsibility, however, is on us, individually and collectively, not on anything we have created or done, not on technology.

There is evidence out there about the challenges we face as we mainstream technology in our lives, calling forth or demanding our responsibility and good sense. In academia, for example, where AI is more pronounced, there's a dilemma, co-occurring with merits. Of course, the dilemma here constitutes the worries more than the merits. Originality, for instance, is wearing thin, as AI is being used to do some of what we would normally do to stimulate and expand our capacity. In other words, we are no longer feeding the brain what it needs for that original flare, resulting in a slow erosion of our natural capacity.

Many positive emotions stem from originality, the human type, which are truly rewarding and edifying for humans. Satisfaction, fulfillment, pride, and dignity rise out of originality, all validating its implication in growth and achievement. According to Ezra Klein, that, sadly, is being compromised in academia. In an interview on one of the news networks, Klein, based on one of his books and empirical observation, asserts that colleges are now facing a challenge of originality, as many students now resort to and depend on AI for research, ideas, and concepts. It's easier now for students to present knowledgeably and expertly on a topic or concept within minutes, courtesy of AI. The problem is that this does not evaluate or measure what the students can do. It seems like a scheme or scam when we embrace travesty in academia by allowing it to devolve into fakery or superficiality. Is this what we want in academia? If this is permitted and indulged, then the entirety of academia will be bludgeoned at our hands. With their dependency on AI, Klein posits that students can be detached from what they are learning and submitting, in other words, not vested in what they present as their work. He further suggests that one of the ways to deal with this is to require students to present and defend their work orally, following submission of the written version.

As an educator, I have also seen how technology has compromised students' performance in reading and other disciplines. I recently sounded off on my observation about students performing significantly below their skills and demonstrated capacity on a district-adopted, online reading test. When I tested students individually and face-to-face, I found that they did significantly better than when they tested online, with some testing three grade levels above their digital performance. I decided to observe students' behavior while testing digitally on their assigned laptops and found out that the students were random and uncommitted while taking the test. They rushed through the test, with some not reading the assigned passages at all. They wanted gratification from another source—games, on their assigned devices. The games were far more attractive to them than the reading assessment. They would rather have fun than show what they knew and could do on the given tests.

Since test behavior was implicated in students' inconsistent performance, I advocated for a more balanced approach. This helped in evaluating students' performance using multiple measures, an approach that uses various and diverse ways to assess students' skills, competencies, and capacity.

There's no doubt that behavior is a significant factor in human performance, and if it is not the appropriate type, results can be invalid. This has grander implications, as our entire life is a test itself. Challenges are inevitable in life and, for example, double as tests. Therefore, the chances of surmounting our challenges rest heavily on our individual and collective behavior, even when superintelligence and AI present those challenges. Again, it is up to us to determine what happens to us—minimizing excuses, sponsoring responsibility in place of abdication, and elevating the decency of our humanity.

As I wrote elsewhere in this book, distractions and challenges are coming at us at a speed and in volumes that are unpredictable and unprecedented, infecting and inflecting our behavior troublingly. It is a world of noise more than substance, a terrain of bickering more than reasoning, a sphere of vitriol that denies peace, a global community that is walking away from itself, a world where disorderliness overruns orderliness, and a world where runaway technology can topple our humanity. Again, how do we better

manage our society in the face of the cresting challenges?

Circling Back to Self

Circling back to the self, myself, I have pledged myself to a litany of things, during and following my recent life-changing bout with cancer. I am willing to heighten my spirituality as described herein, see myself in everyone and everyone in me, and do harm to no one. I am eager to bar biases and put a lid on arrogance to free my mind, believing that sophistication or grandness swells from embracing a balance between perceived softness (humility) and toughness (taking a rational stand on issues). I am willing to frontload gratitude ahead of making a request. I am eager to be prudent using technology, mining it for what can add value to who I am, not what will plunder my humanity. I am willing to lavish my time on my harmless interests that could offer me psychological safety when challenges gather. I am willing to be forthcoming and forthright in my relationships with others, knowing that although reciprocity may be hard to come by, it still pays off for my self-dignity and intrinsic peace. I intend to revere nature in all its spirituality and purity. I am willing to confront my fears and challenges, believing that opportunities sometimes lurk in challenges. I am eager to damn bitterness and cede its place to kindness, knowing that kindness kindles where bitterness darkens. Above all, I'm willing to strengthen my spirituality and faith to fend off anything threatening my fulfillment of these pledges. These were—and still are—my pledges on my deathbed, a deathbed I walked away from, reborn and refreshed, where many never had this golden chance. On that same deathbed, it dawned on me that life is a gift, which we must give back in its purity to deepen our spirituality and faith in Godly terms.

My grandparents and great-grandparents blazed this path. I must not take a different route, for it cleanses, heals, kindles, and rekindles; it is one that delivers that gift of life back in its original form and places my self-worth above net worth. Although these pledges are personal, I can see their relevance in the collective, with our world much more humane and livable in their wake.

Again, according to the Dalai Lama, "It's a miracle you are born at all. So, what are you going to do with your life?" Far from being rhetorical, this question is existential for all of us. May it ring in our ears, play well in our minds, and show up with a meaningful answer in what we think and do to protect our essence of humanity! In a

Circling Back to Self

"Dylanian" (Bob Dylan's) sense, as it gets too "dark to see," we

must open our aperture widely and train our lenses on the essentials

to brighten our future.